THE MEMOIRS OF
SPIDER JACK YATES
... AND OTHER STRANGE TALES

THE MEMOIRS OF
SPIDER JACK YATES
... AND OTHER STRANGE TALES

by

C. A. CHIMENE

1stBooks - rev. 01/26/00

ABOUT THE BOOK

Looking for a fast read with a lot of laughs mixed into your history, philosophy and drama? Look no farther! This is it! In the "Memoirs" you'll meet a true, old-time Texas entrepreneur, one hard to forget. Spider Jack will take you on a fantastic romp around the world with his quaint metaphors from just before WWII trough the "Cold War." Follow him through his wacky meetings with Hess, Goering, Hitler and Churchill. Meet his paramours, Abby Van Cleft and a host of others, and check out his "Texas Insurance Company." His intrepid forays behind the "Iron-Curtain" for Nazi gold brings him to introspection and a desire to retire, get a college degree and travel the world. His parties with the rich and famous in a frantic attempt "to profligate" are a gas. You'll laugh at the depths of his personal "Squeeze," following his Hollywood debacle that left him in the "Bing Cosby home for the erotically deluded." Finally you'll experience his glory delivering an amazing classified report to the Pentagon brass and cavorting with a brash blond.

In "Strange Inventions" you'll meet the improbable inventors, their strange contrivances and sample the epic poetry that immortalized them, as the author mimics the style of your favorite poets. "Short People" will allow you to peer with glee into the lives of these infamous small ones with a clear conscience, as all of their stories have a moral. You'll meet the dangerous Japanese "Tiger of Borneo." The incredible Guy Veaudeaux, a short, French resistance fighter, and famous cork-soaker. You'll meet a real Gnome of Zurich and the Dead Sea Trolls. You'll marvel at the truth behind the famous Hollywood movie "Viva Zapata" and have a brush with real Irish leprechauns. In "Truth Stranger or Fiction" you'll find the fun and how far a search for truth can lead you. Whether he is poking fun at the ancient Greek Philosophers, exposing the mirth in the Seventh Flag over Texas, or telling the hilarious story behind Napoleon's first battle against rockets in 1812, you'll find the author's use of language uniquely enjoyable.

The following short stories: "The Looming Glower in the Gloaming," "The Laahnz" and "Noblesse Oblige" all showcase the author's droll wit and irony, and show just how far the author will go to please you. "The 'Z' File" will whisk you to the future and back through the pages of time to mankind's original beginnings, as divined by all-seeing scholars of the future, in a way that shocks and convinces the reader with its incisive wit and comedic whimsy. Finally, with the Caliph of Frankistan," you'll meet an improbable pair of depression horse-race touts and their zany adventures at Epsom Downs, Houston's first racetrack. You'll meet a passel of quite interesting folk, from little Marvin, the Maestro and sweet Miss Emma Jean to the mobsters from Chicago. Alas, a more comic, yet poignant story will be hard to find.

TABLE OF CONTENTS

THE MEMOIRS OF SPIDER JACK YATES
WORLD WAR II

"Fade you!" I said tersely, dropping a fat stack of greenbacks on top of his bundle lying on the hard dirt surface of the alleyway. "Of course it's impossible," I mused, watching his big blue lips peel away from his white teeth in a straining grimace as he rolled the dice between his two powerful hands. Hell, it'd be easier to sell Gandhi a tux.

He rattled the bones and whispered to them like they had life, sweetly begging the pair to hear and be obedient to his commands. "Seven!" he ordered throwing 'em against the brick wall of the old auto repair shop.

"Snake eyes!" I yelled triumphantly, as the spinning pair came to rest in the dust at my feet. I scooped up the dough swiftly and silently, like a barn owl snatching a field mouse and grinning, asked, "You got any more cash, Blue?"

"Naw," he spat, shrugging, "it ain't my day."

I stepped lightly out of the shadows, walked toward the Macatee Hotel, and kept going past it 'til I got to the railroad station and bought a ticket to Chicago. Hey, they don't call me Spider Jack for nothing. When I see what I want I make sure it's there, and pounce. Ain't many guys can pounce like me. Years ago my old daddy, who lived in the abstract to the point of nonexistence, said in one of his more lucid moments, "Young Spider's pounce is as unexpected as an Indian summer's day in July." What a guy! As mean as noon to midnight, and incoherent as a babbling brook.

It was as hot as hell's attic in Houston, and I had a yen for a certain tall redhead in Chicago. Besides, my bankroll made it obvious to me that I'd already cleaned out most of the turkey-dreamers in town. That summer of 1939 Houston was as slow as a lazy gator lying in the shade. I craved action and figured the big town needed a work over. There was a lot of fast action up there where the high rollers were all pragmatic and as greedy as army ants on the march. Besides, it had been awhile since I snuggled up with Fettuccine Salafumo. She was as mixed up as a tossed Greek salad and as hot as a bottle of green peppercorns. Her dad was one of those tall thin aristocratic-looking redheaded Dagos who fell for an Indian gal, married her and had about a zillion kids; one of the last ones was Fettuccine, and a more mystical yet down-to-earth gal never existed. Just the sight of her, in my mind's eye, walking on the lakeshore in that strong cool breeze, swaying like a willow tree, actuated my prurient interests to their penultimate. We could walk the shore for hours, and she'd never say too much, but when she did talk, her intuition, mysterious feelings, supernatural ideas and weird attitudes clued me that her grasp on reality was as tentative and insubstantial as an invisible Grand Marnier soufflé in the twilight. I liked that! What a contrast she was to her old man. That guy was as predictable as a room full of Republican Marines discussing the National Debt, but as durable as the Ozymandian sneer. The old bugger must be 80 years old.

By the time the train pulled out of the station, I was in a poker game in the club car with three drummers and a preacher from St. Louis. I started the game using my normal method of reconnoitering their poker techniques and habits. I played five-card stud to check the way they'd bet and bluff, noting their erratic and conservative natures with almost all the cards in view. Then after about an hour of that I switched to draw poker, my normal methodology. Now, all the cards would be covered up but they'd just bet and bluff like they did at five-card stud. By then I could read their hands like the cards were marked. It never fails. They got as screwed up as the tools on Ike's garage floor at five p.m. I cleaned 'em five hours out of the station. Not much dough but it felt good just to push them into the losers' circle. I got pushed there once back in '29. Lost a couple million and my damn insurance company when those New York bankers stripped off my pants. I'll start up again one day and put that outfit out of business when I get the jack.

We pulled into St. Louis the next morning. Had a three-hour wait in the station. It seemed as if half the passengers wanted to split for a bottle of that famous St. Louis beer with the absurd name. It was a gray day; the town looked as gloomy as the sewers of Paris: damp dark and with a sweet acrid smell that reminded me of a bushel of rotten peaches in a slop bucket.

The train chugged out of St. Louis headed for Chicago before noon and the next thing I knew I was having lunch in the dining car next to an attractive dish of "someone else's wife." Wilma was one of those prim, typical housewives, married not too long to a fairly successful guy, with more money than sense, who gave her too much free time. She was bored with it all. I figured she'd never met a big shot like me, free for the whole afternoon, and besides I noticed right off that she had a pair of thick ankles.

Now I don't actually remember why or how it all started, but as far back as I can recollect I've always been attracted to women with thick ankles. In fact, a woman's ankles are the first things I notice. Exactly what the attraction is, I don't know. I sure can't analyze it, though I've tried a couple of times. It's probably one of those psychological things that happened to me when I was a kid. I only know that they tip me off that it's time to shine. Now some guys know how to look at horses in a paddock and tell which one's going to win the race, and I could do a bit of that when I was a kid. Sorta talk to 'em, but after the age of eight I lost the talent completely and can't bet the races any better'n the next guy. When it comes to reading dolls with thick ankles though, my ability just seemed to grow and grow, and by the time lunch was over it was obvious to me that she and I would be putty in each other's hands by the time we reached Chicago. I spoke to her as straight as a West Texas highway and as blunt as a letter from the IRS. Her breasts were as round and sweet as little bowls of apple sauce, and her wet red lips glistened, as she told me how she loved her husband and the lives they had back home in Chigger Oaks, but those deep sighs and saucy eyes couldn't lie. I'd heard the same story a hundred times, and it was just like playing a winning poker hand; still, a whole lot of fun.

I slipped the porter a twenty, and before you could spell Benito Mussolini, I was ensconced in a drawing room with a bucket of ice, some glasses, a big bottle of rye, and that soft, sweet smelling bundle of warm flesh. We thrashed around in a hot slippery paradise until the call "Thirty minutes to Chicago" resounded through the cars. Dough won't buy you everything, but it sure has a way of conveniencing your desires.

I spent three months jacking around with Fettuccine and the high rollers in the "toddling town" 'til I had to open some major bank accounts, and felt I'd absorbed enough red-haired hormones to talk like an Irishman. Matter of fact, I passed my 54th birthday up there with Fettuccine, and she fixed me some pie I'll never forget. It looked almost human and kissed me back. That old gal was something special, like the cherry in a drug store ice cream soda or the flying red horse on that Dallas skyscraper.

The next Friday morning I picked up the paper and read that Germany had invaded Poland. "Hot damn!" I thought, "It's back!" I remembered the snookering I took in WWI and hotfooted it to the commodity exchange and stockbrokers. I stuck a bundle in war stocks and commodities and headed back to Houston.

I arrived back on the 3rd of September, and nobody in town acted like anything was happening overseas. Oh, there was a big Bund meeting on Almeda Street, but they'd been having them long before now. All the square heads were moving their pictures of "Der Fuhrer" into their living rooms and talking about the "Master Race." Now that really pissed me off. Hell, we all knew that the only real master race was us over here, but in a few short weeks Poland went down the tube, and those Nazis were beginning to look as tough as twenty-year-old snow geese.

I spent a night trying to figure how I could cash in on this fracas. I decided to trip to DC and hit old Jesse up for one of those R.F.C. loans to start a new insurance company again. I already had a ten-year-old list of all the crooks I could count on in the State Legislature, and it was still about 85% up-to-date. Besides, Jesse's been coveting a certain hotel on Montrose for quite a spell, and I had a sure-fire scheme for him to get it. I'd figured to use it as bait to get a hunk of taxpayers' money from him. We made the deal in forty-five minutes, and by the end of October I opened the Great United States Insurance Company and Trust. Lined up every high-pressure con-artist I could find to start pushing policies. By February I was looking for hot investments to funnel the jack into. The economy was as strong as hyena's breath, and things were beginning to move as fast as a drum-player on

"Speed."

I knew I had to move pretty fast, but the war just seemed to peter out to a dull noise. Remembering my old dad, timeless as a sundial and flippant as a click bug, who told me that one day I'd have to decide whether to be the bat or the ball; I decided to catch the boat to Europe and size things up for myself. I had to find out if this was going to be a real or phony war.

When I got to Paris, I started asking everybody that could speak any English what they thought about the war, but nobody seemed much interested in it. When I pressed the question, they would bitch about the English more than the Bosch and say that they had the Maginot Line to protect them from what happened last time. They seemed to be in favor of fighting a war of attrition against the Nazis, trying to save French lives for the final battle that probably wouldn't come for another five years. They all walked around with long faces until the wine started flowing, but after a few drinks they'd all start singing the blues and crying. They didn't seem to be taking it in good spirits at all. "What's wrong with you guys? Don't you want any glory?" I asked, but they'd just start shuffling around like Charlie Chaplin with their hands in their pockets, scuffing their shoes on the ground while they waddled around in circles shrugging. I didn't get anywhere with them and caught the train to Berlin via Brussels.

I could see I needed an interpreter and hired one cheap at the university after I arrived in Berlin. I'd say they treated "Der Fuhrer" like he was a God, but I've never seen people snap to God like they did to this yokel. I rented a suite in the best hotel in town, started spreading the dough around hot and heavy, and walking around town in my cowboy chaps, boots, vest and hat. The Krauts liked that. They're attracted to uniforms like a dog to horse posts.

I got invited to a big Nazi party, courtesy of the American Ambassador, and had on my best Stetson and boots when I arrived at the Chancellery with my interpreter. Soon I was drinking champagne and talking to Goering and Hess. They seemed interested in the American southwest and asked me how I viewed their "Human Conditioning." I told 'em that I liked it a lot, especially when it was 20 degrees cooler inside.

Goering smiled, "I believe that no reasonable man can be a mechanist, and yet no reasonable man cannot be a mechanist", but Hess said, "No spiritualist can be attuned to the reality outside himself without being attuned to the reality within himself and vice-versa." Then they both looked at me. So I said, "Nothing could be finer than to be in Carolina in the morning." Hess was much struck, and said he hoped to be there soon. He was a good-looking guy and had that far away look in his eyes that stamped him as a real visionary. Goering had on a beautiful white uniform covered with medals but was wearing a big checkered bib around his neck to protect his tunic from falling food. He had a bunch of air force big wigs constantly bringing him plates of the stuff. The guy must have weighed almost 300 pounds. He could really put away the grub. He asked if I would like to meet Der Fuhrer and took me up to him. Hitler was standing half way up a flight of marble stairs with his arms folded across his chest, frowning at everybody in the place. He just didn't seem to know how to enjoy himself. He snarled at Goering and said, "Who iss der cowboy?"

I introduced myself and told him that we had a lot of Krauts in Texas, but he acted unfamiliar with the word. I guess he was putting me on. I started to light up my cigar, and he turned green. Goering said Hitler hated smokers, but I shot back that that was downright un-American. Then Adolph said that I, like all Americans, had no will power. You know, I'd never thought about that before. He went on to say, if he were the ruler of the USA, he'd have all smoking banned at sport's events and public places. "I'd put all smokers in the toilet", he claimed.

I told that smart Alec that when a chicken walks down the street in Houston he gets run over no matter how much willpower he's got, but that crazy paper hanger just laughed and said he didn't know we had so many wild horses in town. I figured that this scooter-brain thinks we live in the "states" like it's still 1910.

Then my interpreter told me Hitler asked, "Haff you henny choose in Tex'ass?"

"Sure, plenty," I said, "I only wear my boots in Europe."

"Do you haff much choose?"

"Hell, I bet I got ten pairs in my bedroom closet; black ones, brown ones and even a pair of white ones. What-da-ya think we're running over there? We're civilized."

When Fritz, my young interpreter, translated this, Hitler looked incredulous. His mouth gaped open, and his little beady eyes got round as rabbit turds.

"You haff schwatzer choose? Mien gott! Vot a mongrel race!" He spat disgustedly. I figured the guy must have gone crazy with the heat and asked, "Don't you have many shoes in Germany?"

Hitler had a crazy smile on his face when he replied, "Ya, Ya, now ve do. A million uff zem, but zoon ha! Hah!"

He was the squirreliest bastard I'd ever met. I felt certain this loony tune had no fuckin' sense at all and wanted to take over the entire world. He obviously wants everybody's shoes! I'd heard about foot fetishes before, but this weirdo took the cake. I sold them all some whole life policies and hopped the train to London via Brussels. Just couldn't get over that pompous bastard. He acted like he was a God damned dictator or something.

On the way home I stopped off in London to see the Prime Minister, but they kicked me out of Number Ten Downing Street when they found out I owned a Texas insurance company. They treated me like a crook, the stuck-up bastards. I did drive out into the country and see Churchill. The silly little SOB was laying bricks on a damn brick wall. I told him he oughta get him some Mexicans to do that job, as he looked much too old and out of shape, but he just laughed and chewed a bit on the end of his cigar. I felt right at home with the little guy. Yes, he was short, but he was plenty fat, and he wasn't no queer bastard like that fairy in Berlin.

He asked me what it would take to get Uncle Sam in the war against the "Narzis." I told him we wouldn't come in unless they torpedoed the Statue of Liberty, but he acted very pleased with that and said it might be arranged. He insisted that I have a drink of champagne with him before I left, but he only had one brand. Something called "Dom Perignon", possibly French and strictly second-rate stuff, sorta a cross between Shiner's and Virginia Dare. I told him to shoot the horse. Then I talked about my meeting with "Der Fuhrer" and he got mad as hell. He said there was no way that England will give any of their shoes away without a fight. "The British Isles make the finest in the world and will fight on the beaches, fight on the hills and fight in the streets to protect their birthright. We will never surrender!" he said, and you know what? I believed him in spite of his funny accent, especially when he heard about how the guy was going to put smokers in the toilet.

By the time my ship docked in New York, I'd already wired in my investments. Felt like I should go to Washington and tell the boys about my trip, but the "Post's" front page was full of bad news. Seems a farm truck wreck dumped a couple tons of kernels on the Pentagon site and the Department of War had just spent $2700.00 for a load of Dr. Scholl's corn removers to correct the problem. I decided to shut up and head south.

BACK TO NORMALCY

Sticky Ann was tall, thin, long-legged and musky, sitting at her desk counting money and checks as fast as a mantis snapping up flies. Not my type, but what the hell, I've got to lose my prejudices sometime, and at 60 that time has come. After all, what do I care if she has long black hair on her legs and a gotch-eye. Anybody can be attractive after a pint of scotch and a beer. Besides she is competent, quick and a fast snapper. What else does a man need? Maybe a little more soft fat to chew on, but hell, you can't have it all in one doll. That's way God made so many different kinds.

The dough is piling up faster then I can invest it, and I'm into everything: wheat, corn, pork bellies. . . and speaking of pork bellies; I got a letter this December from Goering. He's at Nuremberg awaiting trial as a war criminal, whatever that is, and wanted to know if the insurance policy I sold him back in 1940 paid off on suicide. I didn't want to write back and say no. He had a whole life policy for a cool million with my company. Of course so did Hitler, but they never found his body, and hell, we can't be expected to pay off that kind of jack with no proof of death. Actually we don't have to pay on suicide, but I didn't want Goering to know, and I figured that old Fatso might be considering it. I decided to take a fast trip overseas and tell him personally that the company would pay off. If he got hanged we'd be liable, but a nice sweet suicide would get us off the hook. Anyhow, I'd heard rumors he had a bunch of treasures stashed, and I believed I might have a chance to pick up a slew of them cheap.

I got some big boxes of fruit and vegetables from south Texas and shipped them all via Ellington Field, to our friends and allies at the Nuremberg festivities. With a special pass from the military, I accompanied them on the flight over. When I landed, I offered the supply sergeant at the airfield a duffel bag full of silk stockings for a jeep, but he already had more than he could peddle.

I had to promise this crook a salesman's job to get the car, but hell, he seemed like a real go-getter. I drove to the prison compound and found an interpreter to help me communicate with Big Belly.

I met with Goering in the prison. He looked terrible, like he hadn't slept in weeks. He kept asking me if he had chicken fat on his face and accused the allies of stuffing threatening notes in his bratwurst. I told him that I came especially to assure him that the company would pay off double for suicides, as we in the USA have always considered it a heroic and honorable way to go. "In fact," I said, "That is where the Japs got the idea. You know how those little yellow buggers try to copy everything from us." Then I handed him some papers to sign, in case he wanted to change his beneficiary. He laughed and told me not to tell Hess as that goofball went out of his gourd years back. I didn't tell Hermann, but when Hess flew over to England and got captured, I flushed his policy down the toilet.

Goering wouldn't tell me where he'd stashed his goods, but he told me about Hitler's, Himmler's and Goebbles'. They had all the famous statues of Germany replaced at night with new ones made of solid gold, plated with bronze. Only Hitler, Himmler and Goebbles knew which ones for sure, but the way Fatso talked it sounded like damn near every statue in Germany was recast. The sly dog only mentioned the ones in the Russian occupation zones however.

He was a great storyteller though; I gotta admit. His eyes would twinkle when he told a joke. He started laughing and said, "If you have one German, you have a fine man; but if you have two, they form a Bund; and three will start a war. The English are different. One alone is an idiot; two will immediately form a gentleman's club; and three will build an Empire." We were both laughing and so were his guards, so I asked him about the Dagos, and he said, "One and you've got a tenor; two and you've got a duet; three and you've got a retreat." He even told one about the Japs, and man could he laugh, too bad he was headed for the hangman's noose. The guy could have been a lot better dictator for Germany than that turd-eyed freak with the little mustache. In a way, I was sure sorry to hafta screw him out of his insurance, but what the hell, business is business.

He asked what his chances were of getting off this bum rap, and I told him about as much chance as Stalin apologizing for the damage the Russians did to Berlin. "You might have pulled it off if you'd ever told Hitler to stuff it", I said. But he replied, "All the 'no men' in the Reich were already six feet under."

"Well you just got a bad draw," I said "still if I can get a hold of some of those statues I'll see that Emmy and Edda are taken care of." We shook hands and I left. Oh, I slipped him a little something he'd requested, but what the hell.

I headed to Leipzig with some heavy equipment and a group of old Nazis who wanted work. I was out to grab possession of three statues; one of a guy named Luther, a guy named Melanchthon and one named Mendelssohn. I found the Burgermeister, and he said he knew where the originals were stored. I told him "the authorities" were confiscating these newer statues, and we cut 'em up and hauled them back to Nuremberg in twenty-four hours. I bought a big transport plane from the same supply sergeant, loaded it up and headed back to Ellington Field. Within two days I had all the stuff in my back yard and started examining it. The head of Luther was hollow and filled up with precious stones. I later began to feel sorry for the damn Nazis of Leipzig. Not having any of their statues up, so I sent the Burgermeister a check to set the originals back in place, and within the month, he and the townspeople sent me a nice letter thanking me and Texas for being so nice to them. Well one good turn deserves another, I always say. My gold catch was a bit more than 8 tons or over eight million bucks. I sometimes think about going back and hitting up some other towns, but what the hell, why be greedy? I can buy up half of Houston with what I got already, besides, the Russians are starting to act horsey and an Iron Curtain looks like it will soon descend from Stettin on the Baltic to Trieste on the Adriatic.

I wrote Churchill and told him how I felt about the Russians, but he just told me to, "Keep your pecker-up." If I could do that I'd never have time to write anybody.

A letter came from Goering in September 1946. He said he'd been in jail now for almost a year and he hated it, especially the first ten minutes. *The whole nightmarish war"*, he said, *"was caused by a simple misunderstanding in translation."* Hitler never really wanted everybody's shoes after all; just some Polish ones, or polished ones. I'm not sure which and don't much care.

"Don't pay any attention to what the Germans are saying now", he wrote, "just remember what they said back in 1939, 1940 and 1941 before they were cowed by allied power. We may not have won the war, but we will win the peace and take over Europe in the end one way or another." I figured he'd gone crazy with the heat. Germany was a dead duck. Everybody in Washington swore that beer would be the most dangerous thing ever again produced in that country, besides, if we ever got careless with them you know the Soviets won't let them reunify again. They're not crazy. Still I remember what my old daddy told me. "Spider," he said, "remember it's a whole lot easier to kick somebody's ass then it is to stay awake every night making sure he don't return the favor." 'Course he lived in happier, simpler times before we had all those smart guys running the Government in Washington. Besides, if the Krauts start something up in the future, we'll just whup their ass again.

I called Sticky in and asked her if she'd like a raise. Told her I'd been watching her work and felt the firm could afford to give her 85 cents an hour. The poor broad was so happy she started getting dewy-eyed, nervous and kept crossing her legs back and forth until I got dizzy. I got up, patted her on the back and asked if she'd like a spot of brandy. She drank most of the bottle and started perking up nicely.

"Spider", she asked, "how'd you like to pounce on my bones?"

Well I remembered what my old daddy said, "Always take it when someone offers you chicken on a spit; next time it might only be spit on a chicken." So I said, "Sure, sounds better than a kick in the nuts." I guess she'd heard about my pounce.

I've always amazed myself, discovering what an old man will do, but old Sticky Ann surprised me even more. Oh, it doesn't get any better as you get older but it's still great, and Sticky did a few things I consider nothing short of fantastic. I even thought of converting to Catholic just so I'd have somebody to tell about it.

THE WONDER YEARS

I'd celebrated my sixty-fifth birthday by toasting my remaining faculties. Most still work, though a bunch are as gone as Roman chariots and pyramid engineers. Still, like my old Daddy used to say, "Where there's a whip, there's a way," and I still carry the whip hand on my enterprises. 'Course times are changing and old Spider is gonna change with 'em. I can see as clear as the Pacific is deep that new waves are on the horizon. That's where the excitement is gonna be. I'd like to be there too, but let's face it, I'm on the Social Security Rolls already, and I just gotta learn some new things, if I want to keep "eating high on the hog", living in "high cotton", and staying up "high on the totem pole."

On the other hand, I only finished sixth grade back in Twillytown, and that little voice from the past kept nagging at me. Old Daddy could be as obscure and vacillating as a coal-black, day-old, thoroughbred colt at midnight, but one day, "Spider," he said, "remember that most men are like bees; they spend their lives making it but never learn how to enjoy it. "Money," he said, "is the abstract satisfaction of every wish, but a feller's got to move it into reality before it's too late. The true genius badge goes to the guy that learns the art of spending it before it spends him. You brought nothing into this world, and you ain't taking nothing out, so do your best to break even while you can."

Now the old boy did just that. He never made much, but he really knew how to spend it. Seems like every cent went for his hair tonic, pomade, shave lotion and talcum powder; still, when he got pulled kicking and screaming into the black pit of death, every barber within a hundred miles came to view the remains.

I heard of this maharajah that abdicated and ran off to Geneva with about eight million bucks. He spent six million in four years on wine, women and song and not too much song either. I'd been following his new career to see how he was doing until one day I read that the dumb Wog passed with still about a million and a half left in the bank. Not a bad try, but if you want anything done right, I guess you got to do it yourself. It was possible to liquidate everything in a couple years for about 25 mil, so I needed some help in the spending department. I decided right then that the first best step into dissolution and profligacy should be a college degree. Since Rice Institute was right across the street and had a fair reputation for failed investments; I knew it would be the place for me.

Anyhow, I wanted to learn a few things about science, math and philosophy; sorta find out what it's all about. In the past, I wouldn't have given two cents for any of those weird science guys. I thought Einstein was nothing but a cracked Easter egg, but when that A-bomb went off, I changed my mind. It spoke in an eloquence I couldn't ignore. One night I caught myself wondering if matter is or not. If $E=MC^2$ then $M=E/C^2$, maybe matter's just energy but looks like something. I asked my barber about this and that smart Alec said, "Everything is all form and illusion", so I kicked him in the nuts. I was determined to enroll and confabulate, hob-knob and confer with the wizards and put some of what's in those big domes into mine.

I walked over to the Registrar's Office and demanded an audience with the chief. She was a little, old, dried-up lady wearing a black and white speckled dress and black high top shoes. Her thin glasses were perched on her nose like a butterfly sucking on a lily, and she asked for my transcript. I handed her a "G" note and told her to cut the crapola and sign me up pronto or I'd cut my donations and have her job. She got as agreeable as a cold beer on a hot afternoon.

The first day in physics class was a real laugher. The prof was a young snot-nosed kid with a phony looking, little mustache. I told him who I was, and that I was serious. I wanted to learn all about these new fangled physics things, and I wanted straight answers and no bullshit! He acted like I was as welcome as an epileptic fit, but let's face it, when it comes to moral courage these guys are as steadfast as weathercocks.

One day in philosophy 101, the prof said, "When a polar bear kicks up the snow in the Arctic the sand swirls in the Sahara", and asked the class what they got from that statement. I told him it reminded me of an old song, and when he asked which one, I said, "Lovers Woo in China, and 'Stars fell on Alabama'."

The next years passed quickly, too quickly. Some will say that I bought the right to give the valedictorian address. Well, if it's true, it was the cheapest thing I'd bought all year. Still, this was a proud time in my life, so I've pulled out my speech. You can bask a bit in my glory and read what I extemporized to the graduating seniors of my philosophy class.

"Every year a new group of faces like yours look expectantly up to this podium for guidance in the ways of the world they must so soon encounter. Too bad they lack a sense of identity. Still, if you lack the knowledge of whom you are, remember you won't like it when you find out. The high road of 'Western Philosophy' as taught to us by our beloved faculty of pompous, pedantic morons is obviously a complete dead end. It teaches us that we've come to a 'Y' in the road of life. The turn right leads to pessimism, decay, and death, and the left to mindlessness and mass destruction. Can we make the correct turn, or should we tarry indecisively and eat? Can we trust the democratic process and take a vote, or would this be our undoing?

"We have seen through the mistakes of the ancient Greeks, the superstitions of the religious zealots of the Middle Ages, the philosophers of the Age of Reason, the pedantry of the German philosophical schools of the eighteenth and nineteenth centuries. We laughed with ridicule at the modern bullshit of Spencer, Dewey, James, Santayana and Nietzsche until we have run out of jokes. Wittgenstein passed the ball to the scientists and mathematicians, but they dropped it, fretting over its aerodynamics and their poor communication skills. Then they called time out and decided to change the game to things nobody could understand, unless immersed in a barrel of pickled herring in an oxygen-enriched capsule sixty fathoms deep in the Atlantic, or stoned on 'high-life'. Do we exaggerate when we claim that man is an advanced animal? Dare we spread disdain on our fellow limpets? Sure, we can compare our relatives to swine and hyenas, but what about the implicit meanings explicit in the comparisons?

"Our education has been a wonderful experience but can it

explain why Martha Washington called it 'Fudge' and not 'Choc-full-o-nuts'? Did it tell us why Cajuns decorate their X-mas trees with duck feet or why only West Texans piss in their boots? No! No! And then again maybe we just slept through class that day. Some believe we should reinvent the wheel, but its new shape is as yet unpredictable. Once or twice the ancients squared the circle, but their chariots ran too slow.

"Chroniclers of the ancient Orient have reported that long ago near the middle-kingdom, an Emperor stubbed his toe while out walking. He decided to cover the kingdom's landscape with leather and make toe stubbing against the law. He called his wizards to calculate how many cows must be skinned to accomplish this feat. After weeks of wrangling they reported back, the problem could be solved, they said, by fashioning leather shoes for the Emperor instead. This solution was so economical, efficient, effective and elegant that the Emperor decided to become frugal and save the country's money in a vault. He fired his wizards, his servants, his army and all the people working for the government. Soon the vault was nearly full of the riches of the country but unemployment had quadrupled, and the people were starving. The Emperor's enemies attacked, and the people had little to fight for, so the Capitol was sacked; the treasury vault plundered and the Emperor carried off in chains. He languished in a foreign prison, defiled by his jailers and wished he'd stuck to his original plan to leather the landscape and lather the leftovers.

"The moral to governments is that it's better to waste money on the country than to force its people into poverty."

By the time I'd finished the speech the student body had already mostly walked out. The dumb bastards just never got the message, and now I too have forgotten what it was, but not the reason why I got my degree. I was already working on some grandiose schemes to risk money (not mine dum-dum) in wild ventures and start drinking like a fish in a golden bowl.

One day Butch drove me downtown in the Rolls. He stopped at my favorite tobacconist in the Esperson Building to pick up a new shipment of St.Lucia Cubanos, wrapped in Cuba by pretty woman and guaranteed never touched by human hands, though every now and then you'd find a hair in one that would gum up the works. No one could ever expect to smoke a better cigar than those little beauties. When Butch double-parked the car on Travis whom should I see on the sidewalk but Abby Van Cleft? "Abby," I yelled, "come here this instant!" Hah! She responded to my voice like a tiger to a cracking whip. She was still the most beautiful gal in the world in spite of her forty years. Fifteen of them had past since she worked for me as a personal-secretary and brother, could she get personal. She'd met all my demands save one but then again everybody should save one now and then. She finally married some young football star and settled down with him to do all those disgusting things married people do, but I didn't care how sordid and squalid her life had been: why should I? She still looked as saintly and pure as the Virgin Mary except for the mustache and cat eyes.

"Spider!" She screamed back smiling, as she bounced over to the car.

"Hop in baby!" I said, wiping a bit of the excess grease off of my hair, "Let's find a cheap road house and get oiled so you can bring me up-to-date on your humdrum existence. After all, long time no see."

"I never knew you could speak Chinese," she blushed as she hopped in the back seat, crossing her long tanned legs and brushing the straight blonde hair from her forehead.

"Home, Butch! And hurry!" I commanded and the chauffeur responded with alacrity (and plenty of it). On the way home she told me a sad tale about her poor husband. They'd had some kids and everything had been going Jake; then one night about six months ago both were feeling pretty frisky and they started making love. Suddenly Abby just couldn't quit. She seemed to lose all control of herself and screwed him right into oblivion. She promised me she'd never let herself get out of control in the future, but let's face it, the story upset me a great deal, and the fear never completely left my side, except on religious holidays. I knew she would have no mercy in certain situations, so I determined to be on my guard. After all, at my age a man has to be sensitive, gentle, tender and responsive to his condition, still, like my old Daddy once said, "It's better to have a tiger by the tail than vice versa."

We were in the living room having champagne and caviar, after I'd walked Abby about the mansion's ground floor. Suddenly she said, "Spider, this is the first time I've ever had champagne in a frozen beer mug. Don't you have any champagne glasses?"

Well I was dumbfounded. I didn't know they had special glasses for the stuff. I told her, "Naw, I don't have any, but I'd sure like her to come back to work for me so things could be proper and all. She could have the job of personal secretary and decorator with a free hand on the purse strings. I asked if she wanted the job, and she accepted on the spot. She did insist, however, that I move my Picasso of the Virgin Mary to an upstairs-room, as she disliked her mustache and cat eyes.

I figured this would be the start of a beautiful friendship and a way to spend a pile of dough. Little did I know that she was just out to feather my nest. It was September when I finally closed the deal on the Insurance Company, and the payoff check arrived. I cashed it, brought the dough home (all hundreds in a couple of big bags), laid it all out on the bedroom floor and called Abby in. "Lets get nekkid and make love in it Baby", I said, you can have all that sticks to you when we're finished. She really got lathered up. I bet she crawled away with over five "G's." I know I peeled about two off me myself.

I figured it all out in advance. Being not quite seventy I gave myself another ten years to live and socked away a couple hundred thou in Humble Oil just in case I overstayed my time. I put three million into checking accounts around the country and the rest into savings accounts. I intended to draw a few million out of them each year. My rules were simple; buy anything I wanted to eat, break, shoot or wear, and rent anything I wanted to ride, fly, live in or enjoy. I vowed to never invest or give away a penny to anyone without a service rendered. Last but not least, I determined to always overpay a bit for everything.

I started up my spending program the next week. I began taking my friends and acquaintances to lunch and dinner in droves, until I got tired of all the places in town (there weren't that many of them). Each night I'd find an expensive place to go where I could proposition a gal, but this was a terrible disappointment, as I never found one that would refuse my first offer of $2500.00; I'd been prepared to go ten times that price. By the end of the first month I realized I was in deep doodoo. When Abby brought in my accounts, she informed me that I'd actually made more money off my interest than I was spending. This wasn't going to be as easy as I had thought. It would require more imagination, research and planning to blow this sum before the "Grim Reaper" arrived. I was going to have to quit playing games and get serious about this here having fun and spending dough, if I want to be successful and achieve anything worthwhile. It shortly became all too obvious that I was going to have to travel to move any real money. There was no way to spend enough in this cheap town. I leased a custom Constellation and began a grand tour of the world.

THE SQUEEZE

I'd been extravagant, lavish and profligate for years, but I finally got it right, squandering and dissipating my fortune as fast as it could be done. I guess you can tell how proud I am of this work, but I reckon, I was simply too good at it. Either that or I just outlived my time. Well the sad fact is that I'm broke again and at 72 things look pretty bad, but what the hell, considering I am still alive and kicking. It could be worse and will be soon, no doubt.

I've got some great memories though. Those models, movie stars and aristocrats that trudged through my bedrooms by the score; those world class parties I threw in Rangoon, Alvin, Tokyo, St. Moritz, Paris; those heads of state and beautiful people that attended from all over the world. Magnificent!

Who could forget the night in Rangoon, when Lester Pearson and Indira Gandhi kept telling dirty jokes to Charles De Gaulle until the big frog was laughing, choking, guffawing; completely out of control! They were quite a pair, better than Burns and Allen. They just wouldn't let up until Charlie-boy fell down still laughing and crapped all over himself. What a scene! He started demanding that Hirohito be reprimanded for this sneak attack on his dignity, even while he was still slipping and sliding around in the doo. Indira started puking, in her inscrutable oriental way, and saved the situation. What a diplomat she is, of the old school.

I'm gonna miss old Abby though. One night at a big party she locked her legs around the neck of some tall French comedian and he ran off with her. Never saw her again, the slut.

I caught a coach back to the states and ended up in the old Philippine Embassy just south of U.S. highway #10 in south central L. A. writing a pilot for the T. V. "Ben Casey" show. This Casey was a sarcastic, caustic, young, hard working, and deadly serious staff doctor in a large big city hospital, administered by the paternalistic Dr. Zorba. Sam Jaffe, a friend of mine who played Gunga Din in the movies, had the part and liked his role a lot

21

though they wouldn't let him blow the bugle. Hell, I still have a copy. I'll just attach it to my *"Memoirs,"* and you can read it if you like. I know I liked it a lot. It's got "pathos."

I took my script around to the studio. The first thing I saw was a sign. It said, "Ask and it shall be given, seek and ye shall find, but no casting today." Very clever those Japs.

Ben Casey Script

Title: "**Navel Prognosis**"

Scene: Dr. Zorba's quiet and tastefully furnished office in the General Hospital. Young Dr. Ben just entering through the door, Dr. Zorba, seated behind his massive desk reading Astrology Magazine. He looks up and hides the mag as Casey enters stumbling on the rug. Zorba smiles his great paternalistic smile while Casey looks harried, worried and a bit panicky.

Zorba: (Friendly) "Well, well! Come right in and sit down, Dr. Casey . . . What seems to be the, er, uh, problem? Are some of our patients sick, injured, ill? ---- What's the trouble?"

Casey: (Caustically) "Dr. Zorba, I have this case. He entered the hospital last night...I was assigned. He was complaining of severe pain in the lower abdomen, and although I hate complainers, I gave him a complete qualitative and quantitative analysis, utilizing instruments, manual-digital gear, rotary-dispersion, with steroids, tarpons, amino-acids, peptides, and proteins, as well as many less familiar methods gleaned from recent technical journal literature! I tried ecology, pogonophoria, filmstrips, prosthodontics, pharmacognosy, systematic-organic-chemistry (both theoretical as well as applied). I even tried Parliamentary Procedure! But it appears that in the final analysis, I've done very little for the man. Much more is needed . . . much more, in order to arrive at a complete . . ." (Interrupted by Dr. Zorba)

Zorba: (Paternally) "Now, now, slow down there my boy! Ben, it sounds to me that you've done about everything that could be expected of you, us, this institution. Personally, I think he should be ready to clear out, er, uh, that is . . . to be released to the confines of his domicile." (Thoughtfully) "Hmmm, did you say Parliamentary Procedure? Just how?"

Casey: (Ignoring the last remark and proceeding) "No, Dr. Zorba, the chief trouble remains, the man is in a severe state of acute edema of the navel orifice!"

Zorba: "Belly button?"

Casey: (Losing his sarcasm and becoming somewhat shaken) "Sir? I beg your pardon? I think."

Zorba: (Impatiently) "I said, 'Belly button'."

Casey: (Obviously confused) "Baby bunting?"

Zorba: (Caustically) "Noooo. The small depression in the center of the abdomen, caused by the tying off and removal of the umbilical cord at birth."

Casey: (Awestruck) "Oh, yes . . . you know, . . . I never thought of it that way . . . That's wonderful!" (Like a small boy)

Zorba: (Parentally again) "Oh, get on with it, Ben."

Casey: (Assuming his former caustic attitude) "Quite so, Dr. Zorba. Well, what is needed here, it would seem, is a much more complete investigation. I have actually programmed the entire diagnostic series, and to my mind, the very minimum we must do would include the Welsher-Bellview Test-Group Three . . ."

Zorba: (At this point Zorba begins to look at the ceiling, bored, slumps down in his chair, plays with his face and beard . . . obviously disinterested and distressed . . . perhaps starts whistling a little tune or something similar) . . .

Casey: (Continuing)- "We must synthesize his woollen, check the gastrointestinal tract for sugar and sausage content, possibly administer cyclopropane, and trichlorethylene, prior to an attempt . . . AN ATTEMPT, to determine his individual neuro-opthalomalogical conjunctivitis, if any, . . . then a full and complete bio-hermetically sealed specimen must be subjected to the most rigid and vigorous analysis. Minute, even trace-element particles must be inspected by gamma ray, oscilloscopes, paraphernalia, . . . the basic components broken down into their respective molecular structure. We will then have the basis for further studies . . . " (Interrupted)

Zorba: "Wait! Wait! Dr. Casey, I'll tell you what to do . . . Since you seem to be so interested in the patient's navel, his dwadum, and all that kind of . . ." (Groping for the word.) "Jazz!"

Casey: (Breaking in) . . ."I'm not personally interested, you understand . . . Surely . . . It's just . . ."

Zorba: (Pulling rank, affecting a superior businesslike attitude) "Yes, I understand . . . It's just that you don't understand anything about the problems of running a joint . . . er, uh, I mean an institution such as this one. Do you think that we're running this hospital for our health or something? Man, the money, the cost, and the time! Give this patient a aspirin and tell him to go home and play with his own navel."

Casey: (Crestfallen) "But, but Dr. Zorba, the work I've done, the instructions I've given. This patient . . . " (Interrupted)

Zorba: "Forget this patient, his navel, . . . man. We are on the threshold of a major breakthrough!" (Whispering Furtively) "Two weeks ago I ran across an old Indian Fakir . . ." Interrupted.

Casey: "What tribe?"

Zorba: (Ignoring him) "He described to me a method of Navel Organization never previously attempted by Western Man . . ."

Casey: (Interrupting again) "By 'western' you mean?"

Zorba: "I mean the time has come!" (Building to a crescendo) "I have chosen you, you, you Ben Casey! Because of your brilliant mind, you, Casey, shall make the first great navel study since World War II! "

Casey: (Caustically)"Surely, Dr. Zorba, you're being facetious."

Zorba: (Obliquely thrown off track) "Yes, yes, fa-watch-a-us, face-uh-shust . . ." (failing to understand the word but refusing to admit it) "but that is another area of investigation. We'll discuss that later. But back to the problem at hand." (Intensely) "You proceed up to the specimen room on the Third-Floor Annex," (takes a key from the inside of his shirt, from his bosom, then furtively). "Take this key. It will open the fourth drawer on the fifth shelf of the specimen safe-box. A combination cash-drawer, and suppository receptacle. Pluck out the large jar, (my private stock). Check the label that reads 'NAVELS'. . . 'bout a hundred of 'em, more or less," (more excitedly) "then take them out on the patio . . . to the large pond . . ." (becoming almost insanely involved . . . in a world of his own and beginning to sound nautical, like an old salt).. "It's windy today, there'll be a strong breeze a blowin' . . . well shiver me timbers laddie, you take these specimen navels, take off your smock, pull down your frock and throw these navels, in the froth of the flowing, full-fashioned waves of the pond! Then and only then . . ." (standing with a far away look in his eyes) . . . "as you see the <u>Navel Panorama</u> unfolding before your land-lubberin' eyes . . . with your own navel sticking out to sea, only then oh, Casey will you understand the full meaning of those immortal words 'Bobbing on the sea, like a great big flea, The greatest armada, full of fodder gone to conquer . . . will not hanker . . . cram your jack! Into your sack!"

Casey: (Alarmed) "Doctor, Doctor, stop! Don't! Wait!"

Zorba: "Don't stop me now, Ben . . . An army travels on its navel! Dismissed, Admiral Casey."

Submitted by Spider Jack Yates 2/1/68.

The director was as grim and somber as an undertaker, telling me how the skit was too moody and morose for his taste. "A slough of despond," he called it and refused it out of hand.

"Screw you, Sonny," I said. "What do you think medicine is all about? Money and power?" I could tell we had about as much in common as a dog and a log, so I decided to peddle my papers to the French where they not only understand "Pathos" but "Athos and Aramis." Some happy few "D'Artangon."

I thumbed a ride back to Houston and applied for residence at the Bing Crosby sponsored *"Home for the Erotically Deluded."* The weather was summer-like when I arrived in July, so I decided to just retire and live off the fat of your land.

My wing of the rest home was as cozy as a middle school cafeteria at noon. How they managed to design a place where the dropping of a pin sounded like an auto crash will remain one of God's great mysteries to me. They must have determined that the inmates here needed constant nerve stimulation. I sometimes wonder what it sounds like to people with good hearing. I've lived in this pigsty for the last six months, but thankfully it seems more like six years, and I am, I'll admit, well rested mentally, which I attribute to reading only week-old newspapers.

The attendants and managers who run this place all have the IQs of turkey buzzards with temperaments to match. I guarantee we inmates could run it better without our keepers, who are all criminals, homicidals, retards, and sadists. Oh, every now and then we get a sexual deviant (if we're lucky), but they are few, far between and easily satisfied. I've had to have my ears reattached three times in the last two months as it seems the old women in the place are quite adept at talking them completely off. I'd generally do my best to give these ear droppers a wide birth, but once it happened when this old fat babe was giving me some head. How she managed this Demosthenes trick really blew me away.

Things were as boring as a tunneling machine, so I decided to sit down and write my memoirs. What else was there to do? But how long can guys sit around listening to people just jacking with no end in sight? 'Course, most only last about a minute before they're out of breath and pass out.

I started writing about my first insurance company. What an innovator I'd been. I got the industry's "Man of the Decade" award for inventing the weekly payment schedule back in 1912. The buyers, we called them "suckers" then, later we changed the name to *"patsies"*, thought I was undercutting the competition by charging only $3.50 per week for the same policy others charged $15.00 per month for. I was undercutting the competition and making more dough at the same time. The admiration and jealousy in the eyes of other insurance executives said it all. What most didn't know was that this coup had the additional benefit of changing the due date of each payment. The "Eyes of Insurance" were always trying to spy on my chophouse, but they never could figure how I managed to drop customers for nonpayment just a week before they made a claim. I'll let you in on the secret now that the statute of limitations have run out. I'd never open the weekly payment envelopes until the next payment arrived. If a claim had been made, my actuary could never find the last payment. I'd just drop it in the toilet. What a wonderful racket it was. Like my old daddy said, "Better than a license to steal."

I went under during the depression. Not because the "patsies" quit paying off, but because all the company's assets were lost in the stock market or in bad loans to others in real estate or the market. I didn't like doing all that work using up my brain power and skimming from the public when ultimately those fat, mealy-mouthed bastards up north were going to end up with it all anyway. Those big shots always play with a stacked deck, and not only want all of the money themselves but hate to see anyone else accumulate any. Just when us outlanders figure out how to read their cards, those greedy bastards in New York have Congress change the laws on us. Reminds me of the IRS code, "To him that hath shall be given unto abundance; but from him that hath not shall be taken away even that little he hath."

Well as my old dad used to say, "If there is nothing new under the sun, go out at night or wait for the eclipse."

Some nights I contemplated suicide. I'd lie in bed and ask myself if I'd rather shuffle off my mortal coil or shuffle off to Buffalo, but Buffalo mostly won. Besides I stripped three times and never found my coil. Guess I'll dump this place and take over a college, maybe get back into business or become a sideshow freak. Something good like that. Possibly go for the fast bucks and open an auto repair shop or television evangelical show. It's gratifying to know I've still got enough morals left to stay out of politics. Still I couldn't quite make up my mind.

Then something happened that made up my mind for me. It was the preacher. He was a tall skinny guy with a shiny bald dome. He didn't know much about life, but he really knew the <u>Bible</u>. After a few weeks with him, I knew I had to get out of this place and return to the land of the living.

They brought the preacher in about ten one Wednesday night. He was trussed up like a Christmas turkey, screaming like the demons of hell, and generally gave me the opinion he didn't want to live in our place, but in a week or two he quieted down to almost normal, and they let him out of the high security areas. We became good friends after a while, and he explained how he'd been removed and defrocked (and not necessarily in that order) from one of the finest old churches on Main Street for trying to rewrite scriptures. He knew Latin, Hebrew and Greek, and swore and be-damned he'd translated most of his changes from the originals. Still, one night, he admitted to me in confidence that he'd defrocked himself many times in the presence of certain female parishioners that exhibited a certain willingness to get down to a real search for the *"glories of it all."* He told me certain "Proverbs" were misinterpreted because of the wrong vowel assumptions used in the ancient translations of the Hebrew texts. So I'll list a few of his corrected "Proverbs" to give you an idea:

1. Doing abominations in God's sight is stupid! *Wait till it's dark!*
2. They that live by the sword die by the sword, *but rarely by the same sword.*
3. Although goodness and mercy follow me all the days of my life, *why do they never catch up?*
4. The meek will inherit the earth, *but the mortgage will be a bitch.*
5. Though I walk through the valley of the shadow of death, *I may run a bit also.*
6. And it came to pass that the lost Israelites were sorely vexed and suffered a great thirst. Moses led them to a large stone, which he prepared to smite. Suddenly he stopped, saying he had seen a sign from Heaven reading, *"Thank you for not smoting."*

The Preach said he had gotten away with all these, but the one that got him defrocked was when he declared that God had O.K.'d suicide.

" . . . But the Philistines took him (Samson), and put out his eyes, and brought him down to Gaza, and bound him with fetters of brass; and he did grind in the prison house. ---And they did bring Samson out for sport. ---And Samson felt the stone pillars of the house and prayed to God for strength to topple the pillars, and he asked, 'Let me die with the Philistines,' and God granted this wish and gave him the strength to kill a bunch of Philistines along with himself.

"The funny thing is," he said, "I never changed a word of that one."

Well live and learn I always say, but I knew it was time for a change.

THE COLD WAR

The doll was only twenty-one, brash, blonde and beautiful.

Gazing at her naked body in the hotel room, I'd felt hungrier than ever before on a full stomach. We'd been drinking for hours in my room at the Mayflower, ever since she'd brought me the papers confirming my $20 million dollar grant by Congress to do a three-year study for the Pentagon on the "Art of Chicken in Warfare." It was the crowning glory of my ninety-first year. We romped in the sack for hours. Actually, she did most of the romping, while I was doing my best to maintain my breathing style, one of in and out. Afterwards, when I rolled over on top, I felt drunker than a twenty-year-old scotch barrel.

She was higher than a space probe, as I tried to straighten her up morally, and have her on her way, but she was sticking to me as tight as a pocket full of used bubble gum in a steam press. The Cuban panatelas she'd been inhaling caused her breath to smell like sixteen feet down a smokestack, and her body was as hot as the top girder on the Hindenberg Zeppelin. When we kissed goodbye, her tongue darted in and out of my sagging mouth, slicker than the wheels on a sharecropper's truck.

"What a great looking babe," I thought, "but screwier than Daffy Duck's pinworms."

When she finally left, my mouth felt as dry as two miles down a salt plug and filthy as Uncle Willie's spittoon. I looked at my complexion in the mirror thinking, "Muddy as Cameron Parish breakers and twisted as the pillars of St. Peter's." The bed was as sloppy as a ten-foot mud-bog and quiet as a pigeon drop. "Still," I thought, "things could be worse, and hopefully I'll live to see when."

The U.S. had been in the throes of the Cold War for years, and yet its convulsions were still indistinct. No doubt the report called for by this grant required a great deal of weighty reading. Heavier than three elephants and a concrete-truck. But what the hell, my eyes being what they are, astigmatic, far-sighted, bloodshot and bleary, I can't be expected to waste my time reading all that crap. Hell, no! I'm a research scholar. I'll just hire a staff of incompetents to perform that task, like the rest of the hotshots in this town do. Everybody in Government understands this, and what if they don't. Screw 'em! I got the jack, and the authority, I'll just delegate the responsibility. Then I'll have someone to blame if things go wrong - besides, if the Senators or Congressmen bitch, I'll cut down on my contributions to 'em.

The next morning I stepped out of the hotel onto Connecticut Avenue, and found it was hotter than the Terlinqua Chili Cook-Off in July, and as oppressive as the _____, oh! Never mind. I decided that since I was required to be an "equal opportunity employer," I might as well blow this town off and head for Paris, France. There, I reckoned, I'd take two weeks and ostensibly pursue a personnel search for young good-looking French individuals, mainly girls, to do a bit of reading for me. Unfortunately, once there, I found, at fifty francs a crack, the services they performed were not only hard to put into words but were completely unreadable. On top of it all, the girls felt the salary so utterly laughable that many of them choked and we had to "suspend operations" until I'd administered the old "Helmholtz Maneuver" on them. This maneuver was invented by old Doc Helmholtz, a veterinarian who lived on Post Office Street in Galveston back in the thirties, to extract ham bones caught in the throats of houseguests, but I digress, possibly.

I surveyed my remaining faculties and determined they could stand a trip to India, where prices for manpower were more to my taste. Once there, I quickly discovered I could hire the complete graduating history class of 1976 from the most prestigious university in Calcutta for $14.50 per week, which I did and posthaste. I signed them all up, depositing their first three-month pay in escrow at the First Calcutta Bank Trust and Grommet Depository.

What first appeared an insurmountable problem developed when I realized my 145-man crew would have to do all their work Out-doors in the streets, unless I was willing to rent a great-hall for their labors. I located the Palace of the former Mogul of Mysore within two days and was able to lease it for $77.85 a month. I was about to consummate the deal when slyly informed by Mr. Aiyammah Sambahdii, a slick Indian real estate purveyor, that I had to furnish my own soap supply and this would add an additional dollar six twenty per year. Of course the extra expense was out of the question, but just whose I never asked. My dander got up, much to my amazement, and I refused categorically to restrain it. I ranted and raved and ranted some more. After all, it had been years and ranting is a thoroughly invigorating experience. Finally we settled on a compromise whereby all the soap used by my group would be recycled through a series of evaporating ponds to be constructed on an adjoining ten acres of land, presently being used by a legion of untouchables and their adoring admirers to collect lint. This would allow me to slash the price of soap in half, so I accepted this new arrangement and split for DC.

On arriving back, I was called on the carpet by a number of Senators on the Congressional Oversight Committee. They demanded to know why I had hired 145 foreigners for jobs that should have been sprinkled around congressional circles. I attempted to explain the *equal opportunities clause* in the grant, but was silenced and given a severe reprimand by some of the northern Senators, who contended that the law did not apply to Indians, who were already considered *"wards of the state."* Well, you know what I always say. *"Senators is, as Senators does."*

Having the use of the Library of Congress, I checked out a shit-load of books on "chickens" and the "History of Warfare." Every title in the library was not only available, but not one of the books had ever been checked out before. I had them packed and shipped the entire "Kit and Caboodle" of them to Calcutta. This was the last the Library of Congress or I ever saw of them again. I thought, "Obviously, this is the work of the 'KGB'." Whatever that is. So I immediately contacted the head of Military Intelligence in the Pentagon with a complaint (I later discovered it was called the oxymoron department). They replied that this was not "within the purview" of their department but believed it was "within the purview" of the CIA or FBI. I called these organizations and they both informed me that the matter was definitely within "their purview," and for me to never contact the other organization again unless I wanted to spend some time *"twisting in the wind,"* or *"mopping up floors in the big-house."* They even confirmed their directives in writing.

Well, I'd been through that Mogul's Palace and can emphatically state that it would take me an eternity to mop up that place, 'specially since half the floors were made of ordinary all-purpose mud with a special egg-wash glaze used to satiate the flies. Shocked and chastened, I decided to never call either of these agencies again, and, to the best of my knowledge they never called back. Of course, I've changed names, addresses, telephone numbers, and wife and kids, but everything seems to have worked out well since then, I think.

Staying in touch with my charges in India through the mails, I drove to Merida, took up residence for six months and applied for a *"Mexican Passpork,"* one that couldn't be traced, since its corners were irregular and the entire smelly thing covered with boars' hair. One dark moonless night in midsummer I bought an plane-ticket to the Dry Tortugas, but a hurricane had flooded the isle the night before and the name changed to the Cayman Islands I was just in time to celebrate the occasion. I ordered Dry Tortuga at native restaurants but every time they served me one, it was wet.

One year, seven months and two and a half weeks to the day I left DC, I received a notice from the Cayman Post Office that the long awaited package of data had arrived from my Calcutta staff. I walked across the square to the Post and asked where I could pick up my package. Within a flash a number of the local Bobbies had hustled me into the back of a paddy wagon and driven me to the dock where a shipload of documents was in process of being unloaded from the "Tittatstu Maru." The top gendarme informed me, rather stridently, that there was $175,671.82 postage due. I flippantly eased over to the driver and other three policemen, and winking, offered them each fifty bucks apiece in cash to deliver the ponderous mass to my hotel room. They suddenly began to appear agitated and commenced jumping around and hollering at me and actually accused me of attempted bribery. Things were getting sticky until I offered them each a free pair of Levi's to boot.

Later, in my room, much later in fact, after it seemed I had wallpapered the floors, walls and ceilings with documents, I realized I should have sprung for one of those old Indian typewriters, 'cause the entire pandemonium was in long hand of a sort I considered almost English. After six months I'd only deciphered about twenty-five pages of the 2.73 million-page report. I was beginning to feel it might have been a bad deal to hire those Indians in the first place until I happily remembered I'd only paid for their first three months. I fell into a gloomy black funk, which is definitely the worst kind, as I've always preferred the happy pink ones. Nevertheless the black gloom of the funk began to cover my consciousness, permeate my psyche, envelope my senses and smell worse than the Men's rooms at the Texas State Fair. Then in a flash I remembered that no one had ever checked out those reference books. And since they were still considered captives of the KGB, MIA's so to speak, I decided to write the report on my own and fake it to the bitter end; just like the high diver I once saw who did a perfect swan into a damp handkerchief. The excitement of the idea buoyed my spirits and I shifted gears into immediate action of a sort by attempting to lie down and think.

Since I knew the completed document would be classified, *"For Big Shots' Eyes Only,"* for the next thirty years, and as I was now 92, I figured I was on pretty safe grounds but then again maybe not. You see it was the excitement I hungered for. I hungered for it more than an Addict for a fix, an alcoholic for a bottle, an Eskimo for a blubber sandwich or a comic for a microphone.

I finished the project within the week and after making a few spare copies at the local Quik Copy, sent them to my friends and my top lawyer. My letter to him follows:

Zebignose Falus
Law Offices of Falus, Falus, Falus, and Dick
Rockefeller Center - 66th Floor
New York, New York

Dear Zebignose,

Under separate enclosure I have, this date, mailed you a personal copy of the classified document I will present to the Pentagon within the week. As a top-secret document, you should peruse it with great care and file it in one of your secret places, and don't show it to nobody! Since you are one of my overpaid mouthpieces, remember to be constrained by all that's holy in our personal lawyer-client relationship, and treat it in your normal discreet manner. Remember, keep your flapping gums shut, and don't start running off at the mouth about this to the nearest TV anchor. You may note that I mention you within the report proper, giving you full credit for advising me, against my will, to do the things you contended were in my best interest. So if you know what's good for you, you'll keep this whole matter quiet, you no-good son-of-a-bitch!

My Kindest regards to your sweet family.

Your sincere friend,
Spider Jack Yates

MY PRESENTATION OF CHICKEN IN WARFARE, *(Pentagon style)*

Report X1-737346C-DY-661Z555.05
Person in Charge: **Spider Jack Yates,** CCC, WPA, TVA, IMF, FRB, & SOL.

My dear ladies and gentlemen and you military personnel too. It is with bold trepidation and intrepid disappointment that I present to you today the completed work of a study costing your government $19,575,000.00 of the taxpayers' money to date. The study took a team of over 145 people working over two years to finish. Happily, the project has been completed ahead of schedule. And this in spite of run-ins with the CIA, FBI, & KGB, two of which now have me on their most wanted list. All data presented has been bonded by the CEO of the prestigious law firm of Falus, Falus, Falus and Dick, as within the bounds of the original congressional grant, so if there are any beefs, take it up with them. As a private citizen I simply follow their directions.

Now as I know you are all busy individuals, many with definite plans for lunch, I intend to present the basic conclusions and salient considerations relative thereto. The remainder or bulk of the study was converted to semaphore code, courtesy Boy Scout Troop #70, St. Anne's Cathedral, Sam Houston Area Council, Houston, Texas; and will be made available to your designated subordinates upon request.

Recommendations will follow the report.

Background Facts Supporting Conclusion #1.

A thorough study disclosed that the ancestors of all present day chickens developed from a wild stock of six birds captured in South Central Asia by a hitherto unknown tribe of ball bearings (this may refer to barbarians) called "blatherers." This is believed to have occurred during the reign of the famous Egyptian King Zoser in approximately 3150 BC. You may remember him by his sophisticated stone figures, his two tone shoes and big brown eyes.

Now, there it is! Do you realize the significance of what you have just heard? That cuts it! And it should be as obvious as the nose on my face, had it not been removed by mistake by a lousy dermatologist at the Baylor Medical Center. After cursory examination he asked when I'd noticed it. Not thinking the shortsighted loon was talking about my nose, I said I hadn't noticed it at all. He thought it must have popped up almost overnight and froze it off before I realized what had happened. Though it did take him two full cans of freezo.

Let me be blunt. All American chickens have been domestically developed from six basically foreign birds, and these, our chickens, may still subliminally harbor a treasonous desire to return to their roots. I know I had a tree like that once. They may also be forced, against their will; to submit to threats against their relatives in the "old country" and be subverted both overtly and covertly, depending on their innate introverted or extroverted tendencies. Of course, a great deal depends on the present level of *"chicken communication"* attained by the KGB. It has been rumored that Dr. Vladislaw Humongous has a select team working on this problem near the interior Russian border with Uzbekistan or Kazakhstan or somewhere else.

Conclusion #1.

I conclude that these bipedal fowls offer a "weak vessel" for either concerted development or future study, as their heritage is basically flawed, and they can be easily fried.

Conclusion 2 (Background Facts)

Unstable Psychic Manifestations affecting chickens in warfare past and present.

Much of our present knowledge on the instability problem inherent in the chicken when subjected to political pressures comes from the legendary works of the fabled Mons. Mercurochrome du Petite Pois, a nineteenth century Parisian bon vivant, raconteur, and coq au vin Spiritualist. This mystic and pusillanimous Frenchman was variously described by his contemporaries as a libertine, an epicurean, and a voluptuary gourmand. There is no doubt that his intrepid foray into Asia, gathering data on the history of "Chicken Marengo following the battle of Austerlitz," resulted in some of our most precise extant data on pre-reformation chicken psychology. His paper, presented to the French Academy in 1869, was received with unbridled enthusiasm, and for sheer scope has never been equaled. His perverse nature, however, caused such scandal among the citizens of Paris that all copies of his works were destroyed except for the one surreptitiously smuggled to the Library of Congress and promptly misplaced into their pornography section, until I checked it out.

In the travels of this famous fabliau, a number of ancient

tablets were uncovered. A veritable plethora of pre-Sanskrit carvings on one side and well preserved Babylonian cuniform characters on the tablets' obverse, luckily allowed the entire work to be decipherable when under the influence of a bottle and a pint of Cognac. Petite Pois conjectured, among other things, that the first sign of radicalism in chickens could be observed by a dedicated naturalist upon spying two or more of them wearing straw hats of the skimmer type while petulantly strutting around provocatively. To this day his conclusion has never been questioned, and should serve us well. I believe.

Conclusion #2

The unstable psychic delusions inherent in their natures, bodes their use to the free world in sensitive positions, ill.

Background Data on Conclusion #3

The Nazi Connection

———————————————

Herr Eric Von Studebakkar, PHD, SSS, LLD, and KFC presently residing in East Berlin was furtively questioned for twenty-four hours near "check point Charley." The following important information came to light:

Prehistoric scratching discovered in Neanderthal caves outside of Berlin, circa 425AD, depict a troop? (Could be coop) of strident robust birds wearing small army helmets while chicken stepping in coordinated concert. Although Von Studebakkar contended quite vehemently that no concerts had been recorded in Berlin before the sixteenth century. Still, he also admitted their recording equipment was not up to par in those days. Under closer scrutiny when confronted with the fact that the caves were "outside Berlin" he had no intelligible answer, but then again who has? No extant records have been found in the cave areas except for one old Bix Beiderbecke or Clyde McCoy 78 RPM (Sugar Blues, I believe).

The famous doctor seemed quite nervous under this microscopic questioning. He began to perspire profusely when asked about the Nazi connection to chicken soup. It was not until we located the small swastika and chicken head tattoos between his toes that he admitted *Der Fuhrer believed his grandmother Splattke, invented "Chicken soup."* Hitler, he said, had been convinced her recipe was stolen by a cunning Jewish stable boy who changed his name to Molly Goldberg and emigrated. He sneered at us and laughed that Hitler could never explain where the matzo balls came from and would always lapse into silence and appear perplexed when the subject came up.

Conclusion #3

The newspapers would open a major can of worms if we proceeded with this project, and the pro-Semites would have a field day. Better to keep them in their place. Why rock the boat? A stitch-in-time and all that.

Conclusion #4, Background Data

Their Unsuitability in disclosure management vis-a-vis the Cold War. Concerning the fighting chickens of the Southern USA.

West Dallas, Texas, near Arlington, is the last bastion of the pedigreed-chicken fighters and their reputation for savagery, unbridled tenacity and prodigious feats of strength, border on the supernatural. To this day, the hallowed name of Joe "Bunny" Brown ranks at the pinnacle of the list of immortal chicken greats.

Yet, herein lies the dilemma. Originally, "Bunny" received his name after a famous fight in 1909 at the fabulous "Cock Palace" on the city's Eastside. This was the main event of the evening and billed as the fight of the 20th century "to-the-death" between himself and two West Texas Jackrabbits. When he, after 47 rounds, disemboweled the desperate pair, he stood astride their carcasses and began to crow "Coo Coo, Coo Coo." He kept this up for 33 hours nonstop until; he was parboiled by the crowd.

Conclusion #4

Although the stamina and ferocity of these animals make them first rate fighters, you can never be sure just what they are liable to crow about. Hardly a trait well suited to Cold War tactics.

Recommendations:
1. *Cancel all projects of this genre.*
2. *Make final restitution for this report.*
3. *Never ask for whom the bell tolls.*

Feeling elated, full of myself and hot to trot, I called Ashley, that brash blonde bombshell and inquired into her availability for another swinging session at the Mayflower. She asked my present status on the grant and then consented to meet me within the hour in my room. I checked my trusses and smiled.

STRANGE INVENTIONS

The illustrious annals of science are punctuated by grand inventions. They burst upon the world scene with such pith, brilliance and awe-inspiring power that the entire course of human history has been changed. Even the personal stories of the inventors pale into triviality compared to the inventions themselves; sometimes vice versa. On numerous occasions it has been left to the poets of the world to immortalize the panoply of human emotions; the brilliance, heartache, sorrow, frustration and grit of these gifted individuals and their contrivances. Poets have discovered subtle ways of opening new portals to life's finer miracles for mankind. They cast a net of mystic threads that bind them, the inventors and their inventions, into a triangle, a verdant, deltoid copulation of rhyme and form. Certain poets appreciated these rare men of history for the everlasting contribution brought to mankind's march of progress. Even when the invention did not become a commercial success, they were still quick to realize that the inventor had at least made that first step along the dangerously hazardous, even tortuous road to human perfection. They were ever mindful of the many centuries it took between da Vinci's first flight contraption plans and the unmitigated successes at Kitty Hawk.

The vignettes that follow sketch the histories of some inventions, which were not what we might consider financial successes. Neither they nor the luminaries who invented them are household words. Still, we know the inventions today through the inspiration they or their creators conveyed to the poets of their age. Remember too, as you peruse the accounts of these inventions, that many may have been ahead of the technology of the day, and we may find them in different guise in the future. Great ideas, like great inventions, have been scoffed at, in the past, the present, and, no doubt, will be ridiculed in future times. Thus, it is well to note that what may seem absurd today may be honored as farsighted truth and prophetic mumbo-jumbo in ages to come. Only time will tell, and this in spite of its muteness to date, so don't hold your breath, but then again, don't let go of it either. It may come in handy someday, and sooner than you think.

Strange Inventions

The Futron

Invented by Jacques Guegeron (circa 1937). This pre-WW II art deco wonder consisted of a toilet that could be folded down into a bed. Guegeron was inspired by Leonardo da Vinci, who had designed the first "sombro", a hat that could be folded out into a toilet. The only problem with the "sombro" was the dousing users took refolding it into a hat after use. The Futron took advantage of the earth's gravitational effect on a number of strategically placed pinballs to facilitate refolding. It sold briskly for the first 48 hours, until it was discovered that the bed would only accommodate persons shorter than one meter in length. Thus despised, Guegeron spent the rest of his life vainly attempting to rectify this problem, but each two-meter folding bed's toilet only fit elephantine rectums. In his "Ode to the Resplendentless," Homer Ward Mandhaven shared Guegeron's frustration. It seems fitting that these poignant words, marking the international bond between these two previously highly admired personages, are repeated here.

"Ode to the Resplendentless"

Once, whilst feeling, the lack o' my daisy,
I foundered in a less than resplendent futron.
Knowing not what plight to take,
I lathered myself into a filthy froth.
Dumb-stinted, limp-hankered and stilted.
My jaundice spread beyond all recognition.

The Exquisite Alabaster Pencil

This decorator's marvel was first invented in 1803 by Mangrove Swarthout, a seminary student in Salem, Massachusetts, for use in the finest mansions of America and Europe. Beautiful carvings of swans flower blossoms and hermaphrodites graced the highly polished slender stems of each of Swarthout's products. It was reported that President Jefferson used one to sign the Louisiana Purchase, and that he'd sent another to the Czar of Russia to titillate the Russian Monarch's fancy.

The fatal flaw inherent in the design was that it had no lead and could only be used to write on fairly soft substances like mud, balsa wood, wax and gold leaf, products scarce on the frontier in this dry period of history. The patent was pending for many years until it was lost (or misplaced) at the Patent Office in 1858, at which time, Henry Clay, a powerful Washington politician, claimed the invention as his own and reapplied for patent. The new pencils manufactured by Clay's company were inferior to the originals in that the alabaster used was from Georgia and of an inferior quality. Even with restricted use they would crack up within a year. The lovely ornamental carvings were also missing on the Clay variety, and only the utilitarian and cryptic letters "4-Q" were engraved on the poorly finished stems. The pending patent was still pending until long after Clay's death when it too was lost or misplaced.

Walt Whitman celebrated this invention as one *"solely American"*, and lionized it in his *"The Song of the Alabaster Pencil."* Let me share his immortal opening stanzas with you now.

"The Song of the Alabaster Pencil"

Whoever you are holding me now in hand,
Without one thing all will be useless,
I give you fair warning before you attempt me further,
I am not what you supposed, but far different.
Who is he that would become my user?
Who would sign himself a candidate for my
Affections?

The way is suspicious, the result uncertain,
Perhaps destructive,
You would have to give up all else, I alone
Would expect to be your sole and exclusive
Standard.
Your novitiate would even then be long and exhausting.
The whole past theory of your life and all
Conformity to the lives around you would
Have to be misplaced,

Therefore release me now before troubling yourself any
Further.
Let go your hand from my slender staff,
Put me down and depart on your way . . .

His poem goes on and on and becomes even more boring than most. In fact, the latter changes cadence and does not rhyme so well as in the beginning. Whitman later thought the poem too explicit and changed the name to "Whoever You Are Holding Me Now in Hand" and with a few changes and expurgations, made it really bad.

The Spice Island Fork

A Moluccan invention, it was first reported in Europe in the early seventeenth century by Hanzentoes Van Vandeermum. He claimed that during his travels to the Spice Islands he had occasion to actually see an ancient implement formed out of bamboo and black sea urchin spines that resembled a small broad paintbrush, fork or hair comb. He was assured, he related, by particularly high authorities from impeccable tribal sources, that this was an eating utensil invented by an ancient native Moluccan named Muccallagnia Salomandula, also called "Pea" or "Pea Head" in the oral tradition of the area. This individual was thus credited with the invention of the first fork.

The fork itself was formed by two small pieces of bamboo lashed together in the shape of a "T" with twenty-four-black sea urchin spines arranged in three rows of eight each. The ends of these spines, being quite sharp, one must use the fork with care, especially, since it is too wide to place completely within the oral orifice, or any other orifice one may attempt. If used without practice and patience, the fork had a tendency to pierce and bloody the lips of the unaccomplished user.

As the story was related to Hanzentoes, this inventive Moluccan, who lived in the early tenth century, was quite fond of eating sweet peas, but since chop sticks were the only extant eating utensils known in this period, he suffered frustration time and again at dinner. *"Pea Head",* wanting to put more than one pea at a time into his mouth, thus devised this new implement for pea eating. The fork was manufactured and used throughout Molucca until the great pea famine of 1106 when peas became extinct on the island, and the fork, which had always been considered a health hazard, lapsed into a relic of a lost age.

Hanzentoes, never one to inspire confidence, was considered a renegade, prevaricator and licorice eater and, in spite of his repeated protestations, was given no credibility in this matter by the church historians of the day. In Cordoba, Spain, three attempts were made to incinerate him at the stake. He survived this, either by an act of God or an immense bladder. Each time the faggots were lit they were doused from above by a massive deluge of odoriferous moisture that soaked Vandeermum's bloomers from the waist down.

Finally granted his freedom, he returned to the Spice Islands but was seen again only on religious holidays during the rainy season. He never forswore his tale of the fabulous Moluccan fork and according to eyewitness accounts, on his deathbed he mutely raised both hands extending two fingers on one and four on the other. Then, with a beatific smile, he died in a peaceful trauma.

Possibly due to the man's staunch attitude near death, Robert Service immortalized the fork in his famous poem, "The Music of the twenty-four Tines." It is appropriate that I repeat it in this place.

The Music of the Twenty-Four Tines

I recall the bitter Arctic night,
The pea-pickers camp on the trail;
A tiny tent; square of orange light,
Sickly moon above, white and pale.

His meal a-cooking, the stove a 'roar;
Tired, dirty, a blanket his hood.
Though deft with the fork o'twenty four;
Lips red, raw on the snow dript blood.

Downing peas fast as loggers cut pine;
Like back in the land of the free.
Here cold winds blow and the white snow blinds;
While the fork sings so plaintively.

Upon the ridge all bowed down I lie;
And listened with a coyote's ear;
As fork music rose up to the sky,
Casting spells of sadness and fear.

Like that shuttered corral back in Spain,
Where sad ladies cried out their hearts,
And glum Matadors sang soft refrains,
While toasting the dead in their shorts.

I've heard morose songs in the bar rooms,
At operas heard grim divas lilt.
I've heard taps at young soldier's dark tombs,
Dirge singers right up to the hilt.

Still, the sounds that stir and grip my soul
Are the ones I heard on my knees
Where white snow blinds, and chill-frost blows,
From the fork of Moluccan seas.

The Invisible Cloak

The chance meeting of Mao-long Song, a parsimonious Chinese personage, who made his way east to Boston on the recently completed cross country railroad, with Josiah Absalom Drade, famous Boston tailor and inventor, sparked the invention of the renowned invisible cloak. Mao was in possession of a large suitcase of silkworms that had previously been smuggled out of the Far East, and Absalom Drade's hobby was the raising of spiders for their silken webs. He had been trying to garner sufficient web material to make a new kind of cloth, sheer enough to compete with silk.

The two men perfected in 1884 a method of combining the spider and silk worm strands in such a manner that enough threads were available to construct a bolt of cloth 10ft. by 10ft. They fashioned a beautiful cloak graced with gold buttons, which they intended to present to President Benjamin Harrison to wear at his inauguration in 1889. Within twenty-one days of the cloak's completion, it lost the property of reflecting and refracting light and became completely invisible. Only the gold buttons could be seen as it hung in the store window with the sign above it dedicating the cloak to president-elect Harrison who, incidentally, was a Republican and elected in spite of garnering fewer popular votes than his opponent.

The tailor's window attracted large crowds of people, and so did the tailor's widow, but that is another scandal. Mao had to constantly pull on various parts of it so curious onlookers could watch the gold buttons move, seemingly floating in midair. The cloak became the talk of the town, and many college professors signed affidavits attesting to the cloak's invisible properties. Unfortunately the president-elect was advised that the cloak had gained such notoriety that it might detract from Harrison himself, so he refused to wear it. Both Mao and Drade were devastated and, as spring approached, they noticed numerous flies now floating around amidst the golden buttons on the invisible cloak. At first Mao tried plucking them off with chopsticks but, by June, the cloak was literally covered with bugs. There was something within the spiderweb portion of the weave that attracted them and, no matter how hard the pair tried, neither could figure a method to cure the cloak's affliction.

Both men were cursed and derided by the townsfolk and went to their graves paupers and failures. The cloak was burned as a public nuisance by the angry townspeople in 1890. This sad tale prompted John Greenleaf Whittier to write one of his last and most infamous poems. The poem was banned in Boston.

"Absalom's Mao-Cloak"

Of all the cloaks since the birth of time,
That's sung in story or told in rhyme,
Covering Jupiter's golden ass,
Or Catherine the Great in snowy mass;
Cloak of our lord, Demetrius won,
Or gold of Pharaohs, spread like the sun.
Still, the strangest cloak, known to be made,
Was one fashioned by Absalom Drade.

    In Boston town, where he worked out his heart;
    Spat upon, cursed, run out of the mart.
    Thus, the shameful fate of Absalom Drade!

This wonder of worm and spider spun,
With lovely buttons of gold, 'twas done
In such a manner that none could see
The beauty, wealth and wonder of thee.
A fine blending of the ancient East;
The gift of Mao Song to freedom's feast,
With spider-like silk from Drade's own bones
The western world breached to Heaven's throne.

    T'was Boston town, where he worked out his heart!
    Spat upon, cursed, run out of the mart.
    Thus, the grievous fate of Absalom Drade!

In 1870 it all began.
When Mao Long Song stole from out of town.
From old Cathy a long trek he took
With a bag of worms, his home forsook.
He vowed a long trip to Freedom's land,
He'd begin anew in New England.
From Shanghai he sailed in bright sampan
To Malay, where natives ate from cans.

But Boston town, where he worked out his heart!
Spat upon, cursed, run out of the mart.
Thus the grievous fate of Absalom Drade!

The old Silk Road was a danger still,
And kept Mao upon this briny swill,
And so two years past until his fate
Brought him close to home, the Golden Gate.
The railroad, resplendent in the sun,
Captured heart and eye. *"But, how it run?"*
He labored and languished till the day,
He'd saved enough for his passageway.

To Boston town where he worked out his heart!
Spat upon, cursed, run out of the mart.
Thus the grievous fate of Absalom Drade!

Unfortunately Whittier's poem goes on for 375 additional stanzas and cannot be fully repeated in this space.

The Pulviolava

A fastidious individual, Diurnal De Saussagio, the famous Venetian Inventor of the early 19th Century, devised a combination umbrella and douche bag that he dubbed the "Pulviolava." It was designed to capture rainwater while the user was out in thunderstorms and through an ingenious network of small leather pipes, deposit this pristine fluid in a furry bellows. The douche mechanism could be activated, following the insertion of an ivory nozzle mimicking the shape of a rhinoceros horn. It was complete with a major indentation to prevent slippage if the subject happened to be prancing or hopping up and down, and this proved to be a weak link in the invention's popularity, as many Venetian ladies experienced an extremely painful removal problem when rectal use was required.

This drawback was corrected on newer models but the lightning problem could never be overcome, as the tall metallic frame of the contrivance had a decided lightning rod effect when the douche horn was inserted, which at times caused devastating but sometimes miraculous results to the subject. Although originally praised by the Pope, the invention was placed on the index within five years of its first public offering. Later, sales were made in Protestant countries where it was advertised as a drinking water collector but, as commerce languished, De Saussagio suffered a small mental setback and was forcibly institutionalized for the next forty years.

Evidently a shipment of these contrivances found their way to India where they were mentioned in one of Kipling's more obscure poems.

"The Pulviolava"

When the desert calls ye on it,
　　Then us troopers find no rest,
For the blinking mirage blinds ye,
　　And ye know they 'spect your best.

Barren days pass slow and weary,
    Devil sky grows hot and dry.
Till the drops from your cantina,
    Shout, "Within a day you'll die."

Ye can see ol' Marsters weaken,
    Tumble down the sandy berm.
Ye can feel your colt all shakin',
    Jog yer salt encrusted arm.

Slowly clouds appear and darken,
    Soon your heart beats fast as hell,
Ye scream for your Pulviolava,
    Praying that the heavens swell.

Ye quick and check out them leathers,
    And that furry bellows dry,
'Cause ye hope that just like tear drops,
    Rain will fall from out the sky.

Sudden thunder cracks the silence,
    Then the cool wind rushes past.
Can ye see umbrellas blossom,
    Ivory horns stuck up your ass.

Crash! The lightning flashes brightly,
    Sergeant Chalmodelay all aglow,
Care ye not if life's a'fleeting
    Long as water starts to flow.

Loverly, it's all a'raining,
    God's great bounty from above;
Then ye know that you'll survive it;
    Kiss again your ladylove.

Piss-in-Boots

This classic quasi-medical device holds the distinction of being psychology's first contribution to the world of inventive genius. Dr. Franz Garibaldi Krupp, a contemporary of Karl Jung, Richard Von Krafft-Ebing, and that famous group of psychiatrists of the Freudian school residing at this time in Zurich and Geneva, Switzerland, records in his books on abnormal sexual behavior a clinical analysis of a woman referred to variously as Mauzy P and Shiksa #12. Quoting from his study:

Case #12-Mauzy P., 23 years, a strong handsome, blonde, blue-eyed, peasant from southern Austria, appeared in my office complaining of consistent delusions when out in crowds. Her skin was clear, except for one minor unsightly carbuncle about the size of an eyeball in the middle of her forehead and from which, she believed, she could see at night. This was not her main problem, however. Shiksa #12 was born the third child of a farmer and his wife who lived a few kilometers east of Vienna. Her family relations appeared normal with the usual incestuous advances made by the father and two older and one younger brother. All sexual acts involved fit the normal description of a tainted individual of dull intellect and normal mental faculties for the area. Evidently most of Shiksa #12's childhood was spent plucking chickens and satisfying her relatives' clumsy advances, which she enjoyed, at least as much as the chicken plucking. In her seventeenth year she moved into Vienna and became a domestic in the household of Baron E., one of the few untainted families in the city. Between a fortnight and two weeks she developed the problem of uncontrollably urinating in public, sometimes at dinner service and during periods of long continued waiting on family members. The Baron's family, however, took this problem in stride and seemed not too displeased with the phenomenon. I questioned her closely about these incidents, and all appeared to be triggered by the same mental aberrations. The following is a typical story of one of these incidents. The story is hers. The markings and punctuation's are mine.

One day on a <u>Sunday</u>, I was on my day <u>off</u> <u>and</u> <u>went</u> for a jaunt in the park with a boyfriend whom I had met bringing each week's supply of <u>knockwursts</u> to the Baron's estate. He was a <u>fast</u> worker and within a month had asked me to accompany him for a walk in the park. He was tall and quite handsome and reminded me of <u>my father</u>. We walked to the <u>top</u> of the <u>attractive prominence</u> at the park and were standing on the <u>crest</u> when I had this sudden <u>urge to urinate</u>! I knew we were at least ten minutes away from a public <u>debasement</u>. I looked around and saw that no one was present but Gunther and myself, and as he was holding my hand, which I was loath to unclasp, my mind went into this <u>whirl</u>!

"I rationalized, while we were both looking at the beautiful panorama <u>spread out</u> before us, that I could take my free hand and unnoticed <u>flip</u> my underwear aside, then by <u>spreading my</u> <u>legs</u>, ever so slightly, urinate while standing there talking to him and he wouldn't notice a thing. This I did, but half way through I felt the fluid running down my legs, wetting my dress and heard the <u>sound of it hitting the dirt</u>, pooling up beneath me and causing a massive yellow stream to <u>run down the hill</u>!!! Gunther noticed what I was doing almost immediately, but by then <u>I</u> <u>couldn't stop</u> and had to fully empty my bladder. Simultaneously I now noticed that we were standing in the midst of at least twenty people, all of whom took note of my action and many of whom commented sarcastically about my lack of decorum. Gunther was <u>mortified,</u> and I was <u>devastated</u> on being so completely <u>found out</u>. Especially after being so certain I could <u>pull it off</u> in secret.

"<u>I</u> <u>tried</u> <u>my</u> <u>best</u> to consider my <u>action</u> in this highly upsetting time, but emotionally <u>I could</u> not <u>come</u> to grips <u>with it</u>. I kept putting it off <u>over and over again</u>. A few weeks ago <u>I</u> <u>could wait no longer and decided to come</u> to see you and <u>have it</u> <u>all</u> <u>out</u>."

She told similar stories on at least twenty separate occasions, while I examined her private parts. She is obviously the victim of her own dissembling, which she believes is reality until it is too late. After many hours of thought, I devised a crotch-shaped funnel with a long rubber tube leading to a rubber bag that could be attached to the inside of the subject's boot. The rubber tube was secured to her leg with adhesive tape and the funnel held in place by a series of leather straps. I dubbed it "Piss in Boots," metaphorically alluding to the fairy tale "Puss in Boots," another fantasy of the mind. Next, I assured Mauzy P. that she could cease her dissembling, as she should now have no future worries in regard to her "problem." I advised her that a six-month period in this contraption would break her cycle of worry and cure her. Realizing how common this problem was in the area, I applied for patents in Germany, France, England, the northern USA and all countries where this malady is known to present a major problem.

Leaving Dr. Krupp's narration for the moment, it must be said that he informed her employers of both the diagnosis of Shiksa #12's mental state and of his inventive cure. He proposed to them that they place her under strict observation the next time they had a weekend party of at least fifty or more guests and have her working in the guest's presence, around the clock, if possible.

The Baron and many of his family and guests reported back to Dr. Krupp within the month. They complained that his invention was an unparalleled disaster, as Mauzy P. peed all over their prized Kerman, their prized credenza and their prized wooly-booger with such élan that a small toddler floated completely out of the sitting room and into the basement. On hearing this information, the good doctor acted with staid aloofness and considered the Baron and all present to be suffering some new type of mass delusion. No matter the evidence of the myriad eyewitnesses, he refused to even contemplate the possibility of any failure in this matter. Time passed, but whenever a colleague confronted him with facts about the failed invention, he apparently reacted as if he were either not there or had been asked the time of day. He would then mechanically cock his head to one side, nod just a bit and say "10:45 on the dot!"

The fury in Psychiatry circles caused by the psychiatrist's

delusion died down as the months passed and Krupp was restored to prominence. Appointed president of the university in 1912, he remained in this position for twenty-two years. He quit when he was seventy and moved to Berlin to study a massive outbreak of coprophagi in the Nazi party.

Edna St. Vincent Millay penned a passing ode to Shiksa #12 and the Piss-in-Boots contraption in the early twentieth century. Although the poem was unpublished, it was short and to the point and is repeated here in its entirety.

"Pisser Mortuus Est."

Chaos' blossoms cover even kings:
    Mauzy's Pizen boots, hurray, hurrah!
Holds center stage, but presently brings
    A shock! Behold, les deluges c'est moi!

Unremembered but as old rain;
    Now straining her stranglehold of care,
With the succinct metaphor of pain,
    Just an annotation of despair.

Though most all inventions should be good,
    Sadly, this one's no longer cherished.
But now should we say, "It was not good?"
    Only just because it has perished?

Subsurface Band Instruments

Matsuko Nakayama (1890-1953) was a California native truck farmer residing near Carmel just south of San Francisco. His father had a number of Koi, which were family pets and lived in their pond, an arm of which extended within the house itself. Matsuko's father was very fond of them and had learned how to communicate well with them in Japanese. Matsuko conversed, sang and played with them since childhood. By the time his father died in 1910, many of the Koi had been household pets for over 40 years and knew each family member intimately. Matsuko was a true music lover and determined at an early age that almost all of these Koi were musically talented and could play in any band if the correct equipment were available. With the help of an old proctologist, and a theoretical music professor, Matsuko fashioned a number of musical instruments that could be played underwater by his fish, and ere ten years had flown, the final three saxophones were correctly tuned for his willing and waiting saxophonists. The completion of these three instruments finalized his nine-piece band; three saxophones, two trumpets, one trombone, piano, set of drums and bass.

Other than a decided bubbling stream sound in the background, the music sounded easily as authentic as most of the bands then playing in the general area. Oh, occasionally if the harnesses on the instruments were incorrectly adjusted, they would sound out of tune, but as the years passed, the band improved until Matsuko began inviting his neighbors over for Friday night jam sessions. There were problems encountered during rehearsals because the Koi never learned to read music. Matsuko could only teach them new melodies by playing phonograph records to them over and over, until they caught onto the new tunes, and even then the Koi never seemed to learn how to improvise on their solos, so sometimes the music had a decided mechanical cadence. Nevertheless, many listeners from the neighborhood said the sound compared quite favorably to Guy Lombardo's. The stalwart of the ensemble was an old Koi of about 65 years who played the piano. He took to it wholeheartedly and played ragtime with gusto. Whenever he played a rag tune, he would always find a small brown stick to clamp between his jaws, mimicking a cigar stub, while he played and rolled his eyes. The drummer and bass player were the only fish in the band that could keep up with him when he was "ragging"; the others, the trombonist, trumpet players and three saxophonists just floated around the pool looking stupid during the rag sessions. Try as he might, Matsuko could never devise a clarinet that sounded right underwater and in later life bemoaned this fact incessantly. Neither did he ever patent the instruments. One may only conjecture the reason for this neglect. Possibly he never foresaw any mass use and considered his band a salient phenomenon.

Matsuko was a perfectionist and finally settled on a repertoire of some forty tunes he considered great American favorites; from *"Ragtime Sal"* to the *"Marine Hymn"*, from *"Give My Regards to Broadway"* to *"Somewhere Over the Rainbow,"* from *"Sugar Blues"* to *"Star Dust"* and *"Skylark,"* from *"Marie"* to *"Moonlight Serenade."*

When he felt the band was ready, it was late 1939, and he began searching for an agent to come out to his pond to listen to the band, but most beefed in reply to his queries that there was no way to put his show *"on the road."* Things went slowly, and it was not until the middle of 1940 that five agents actually made the trip out to listen to the Koi band.

Two complained strongly about the acoustics and the cricket noises in the background, and one was adamant about the color of the trombone player. Two felt too many of the songs were out of date and were dismayed at the omission of any popular "boogie-woogie" tunes. Four felt the lack of a vocalist was an insurmountable drawback. One agent however, believed the group should be given a *"break"*, and said he would contact the recording studios in Los Angeles and attempt to "crack a deal."

Final contracts were actually signed December 5, 1941, and preparations were being made to transport the latest recording equipment to the pond within the month, when the Japs bombed Pearl Harbor. This unfortunate attack, (now known to have been due to a slight misunderstanding in translations between two peaceful neighbors on the Pacific Rim), came at an alarming time for the band. It seems a few RCA executives sensed that the debut of a new Japanese band might be considered untimely at this particular date. Consequently, in a close vote, they decided to delay the recording of the first album for six months.

Grievously for music-lovers coast to coast, the California National Guard arrived within this six-month period and carted poor Matsuko off to a resettlement camp in Montana for the duration and six. By the time he returned to his pond after the war, all he found was a major concrete freeway and a high rise luxury condo. Sadly, Matsuko constructed some little origami paper boats with pictures of drums, bass, piano, trombones, trumpets and saxophones on them. He lit small candles on their bows and sailed them down the gutter during the next rainstorm.

The pathos of this ceremony was captured in a poem immortalizing the "Famous Koi Band" in 1973 by an anonymous poet (rumored to be Hirohito himself by certain well placed Japanese aristocrats). A plaque commemorating the pond was placed on the side of Condo Building Number Three, which was evidently built on the pond's original site.

"The Twilight Hush That Fills the Land"

Oh lovely strains of music land
That lends us thrills emotion packed;
Some soft, some brash, some sweetly rand,
Universal life our universe still lacks.

O' Koi that play within the pond,
That music wafting so serene,
The Royal Crane still hears your beat
From Carmel by the sea to old St. Pete.

Can I but hear one last refrain?
Of "Ragtime Sal" or "Starlight Serenade"?
Will "Moonlight Cocktail" muteness stain
Sad memories of that midnight raid?

O' Koi that play within the pond,
O' music wafting so serene,
Miraculous deeds that you have wrought
In land of sun forever will be taught.

To never hear such pure of heart,
The music fish of way back when.
Must we all bear this loss and part?
When U.S. thugs took one, killed ten?

Oh Koi that played within the pond,

A twilight hush now fills the land,
So nevermore you'll play, just rest
Beneath cruel concrete's rumbling crest.

Then one last candle ride will come.
Matsuko's navy 'twill pass the test,
May sail them up to heavens blest,
And treat the Gods with fishes' best.

Oh Koi that played within the pond,
What was your fate in freedom's land?
Can you nevermore complete the score?
Will freedom's flag fly unstained as planned?

Take one last look down memory's lane
Remembering all those gay refrains.
The beauty of sound - the trumpets crash -
The trombones blare - all gone to trash.

No Koi yet plays within the pond,
A twilight hush now fills the land
But, forgotten they will never be!
For bright Sun Flag flies on condo three!

The Möbius Chair (1819-Leipzig, Germany)

This is an example of one of the rare inventions that can be said to have been "after its time." It was invented by the famous German theoretical astronomer and mathematician August Ferdinand Möbius. He was born in Schulpforta, Prussia in 1790 and became the professor of astronomy at Leipzig University in 1815. By 1817 he had developed the Möbius twist that could turn any two-sided surface into a one-sided one. He realized, almost immediately if not sooner, that by applying a half twist at the corners of a hat, similar to the one made famous by Napoleon, it would change into a perfect field chair. Thus, he was inspired to create or invent the first combination hat and chair. Of course, the hat had to be formed just a bit larger than the one Napoleon used, but he considered this no drawback to the project.

He spent his off-hours fashioning these hats in secret in his basement with the help of his wife Cöitus and, within a year, began a marketing campaign of his stock of 7,903 hats. He had previously gauged the chapeau and furniture markets using the scientific method and constructed the hat-chairs in beige, pastel blue, forest-green and basic black.

Napoleon was, of course, a personage of tremendous esteem when Möbius was a young man. The French ruler was a style setter throughout Europe, Haiti, Mexico, Brazil and Madagascar; however, he had now been incarcerated for the last few years on the Isle of St. Helena, and this Napoleonic hat style had gone decidedly out of fashion. In spite of the public's original admiration of the field chair and its wonderful convenience in transport, the hat style became a major drawback to the item's sale, except to certain groups of Frenchmen in Dijon and the Haute Provence.

Adding misfortune to Möbius' exploded invention was the frightening rumor circulated around Prussia and West Germany that a person was sitting on the chair when it spontaneously collapsed and re-twisted, with the horrifying result that the person caught sitting in the chair lost one of his dimensions. We now know that, thankfully, it wasn't height, but whether the afflicted one lost width or breadth is still unknown. Within a year, all of the hat-chairs that could still be found were burned in effigy, until none remained within the borders of the Germanic states.

This failure shattered August's inventive fortunes and, for monetary reasons, he was forced to remain a college professor for the rest of his natural life (a shameful fate for a resourceful man). The only bright spot in this sad, short-lived, and humiliating experience was the invention's immortalization by Percy Bysshe Shelly in his final poem, written in 1821, which he entitled in French to disguise its impact on the already ridiculed Möbius. It is appropriate that this poem be repeated here for your enjoyment and edification, as it is considered one of Shelly's best and lends us an example of the power and beauty engendered within a blighted mind.

"O' Möbius Chaise Chapeau"

I traveled from an antique land to France.
A chair of light and grace did come to view.
Beside, half nestled in the trees, a lone
Frenchman stood, whose tears and quivering lips
Shaking chin and sobs of sad refrain,
Tell that the grievous one full these unhappy
Passions racked - as he but stared upon the
Chair-turned-hat that "well loved" Möbius wrought
Optimistically, when but his muses sang,
To place the great Napoleon Chapeau
Upon the heads of Earth and seats of Kings!
Yet greater still, immortal fame did call!
Strangely, time, as of a point that's passed,
To which no person may again return,
Demarks an age of greatness that will never
Come again to cloud our minds, our body's
Passions and our hungry heart's desires
With twilight dreams. Alas, it's fashionable
No more! No glory yet surrounds! The aura
Shrank and wrecked the dream of mere mortal man.
Fly! Cease to be! Leave not a track behind!
Lone and beige the chair-hat fades soft away;
Is seen no more and evermore vanishes.

The Infamous Two-Man Saxophone - (Circa 1884)

Of course everyone knows that Antoine J. Sax, also known as Adolphe, invented the first saxophone and had it patented in 1846. The saxophone was an immediate hit in musical circles because the fingering was relatively simple and it had a lot of little valves and cute little leather pads all over its shiny body. However, Adolphe was a French speaking Belgian or what is called a Walloon. The invention caused great jealousy among the ranks of the Flemmish who purposely, at this time insisted on a double "m" in their name simply because the Walloons had a double "l" and double "o" in theirs. The Flemmish invoked a town meeting in Antwerp just three weeks after the annual Twerp Festival and voted to have Henried Von Maastricht invent something twice as good. He did, after all, have a double "a" in his name and this seemed a portentous omen, although the Flemmish had no faith in portentous omens and preferred omens of a far more trivial nature.

Try as he might, Henried seemed incapable of inventing anything new. Meanwhile Sax invented the sax-horn, the saxo-trombo, and the sax-tuba. Then in 1857, the same year that Sax moved to Paris to assume the Instructorship of Saxophone at the Conservatoire, Henried hit upon an idea, though it hit him first. He decided to make an instrument twice as good as the saxophone, a two-man saxophone that could play both melody and rhythm like a piano. He perfected the instrument, and it was an instant success. Two sax players together could make wonderful music but had to practice in duet, and this became the invention's Achilles heel. If someone wanted to learn to play this instrument, he needed to find a partner of the same persuasion, talent, and who lived nearby, so the pair could practice simultaneously. No one could learn the dual or double sax on his own, as when one blew, during certain passages, the other had to suck. Consequently, the most compatible partners were members of opposing sexes, and even then, certain Belgian women of the period preferred to blow instead of suck, and vice versa. Thus the double saxophone had limited popularity, especially with the Twerps, and was soon abandoned in favor of the "French kiss" which, though less melodious to the ear, nevertheless was apparently more satisfying to the soul.

With strident exhilaration, none other than Der Fuhrer himself wrote a poem praising this Flemmish accomplishment, and although its translation into English may leave the poem a bit ambiguous, I believe it still succeeds in capturing the essence of Hitler's feelings of good will toward the Flemmish people. Certain critics felt the poem revealed some possibility of subtle, dark and shadowy undercurrents of perceived non-Aryan racial overtones that Hitler may have felt toward the Walloons. However, this latter is merely equivocal and may be due to translator error. "Der Maastrichtphone" was written in 1928 and in modern times it is only prized in remote areas of Eastern Germany and Vienna where they perceive it has beneficial effects on their sausage. Still, it was considered Pulitzer material in 1929 for its emotional impact and tenuous nationalistic overtones.

"Der Maastrichtphone"

Und now ve finds der *"Holy Grail",*
For Vallooners are der vons who'll fail.
Heil to this doppelganger sax;
It is Aryan to the max!

Ve Nazis mit der Flemmish crowd,
Haff reason now to be quite proud.
Ve play "Deutschland Uber Alles"
Humph, Paris it's Bergere Follies.

Ve'll show ve are der Master Race,
Mit Maastrichtphones to set the pace.
Der filthy Vallooners think they're schmarts,
But ve'll be there to break their hearts.

Verstunkers! Scum! Yah everyone!
Ve'll blow them all to kingdom come!
Vhen they come whining on their knees,
Ve'll make them wash our BVD's.

So Flemmish hold your heads up high,
Immortal Maastricth's vill not die!
Ve'll dredge the Valloons' sax in dreck,
Und hang them by their scrawny necks.

This inspiration for our race
Commands us to keep up our pace.
Ve'll drag that Valloon sax through Frawnce
Und hang them by their scrawny schwance.

Paper Money (Circa 111 AD China)

The invention of paper money is credited to a Chinese person named Hot Suey, an advisor to the Great Chan, Emperor of the Middle Kingdom. The Great Chan wanted all the gold in the land put in one room. This room was constructed by order of the Great Chan, who inscrutably entitled it the "silver room." It was then decreed that only gold would be accepted for tax payments for ten years, and all commodities presented were exchanged for gold at the then present rate of exchange, so that it may be taken to the "silver room." As gold became very scarce throughout China, its purchasing power increased until a law was passed that no citizen could own any gold, and all had to be turned over to the representatives of the Chan. Within a few years the Great Chan had all the gold in the country within the silver room and his sage, Hot Suey, came to him and said, "We now have all the gold in the Kingdom safe within the 'silver room.' Would you like to come see it?"

The Great Chan went into the room that was filled with gold, and he loved it. He spent most of his days playing with it and determined that it was his forever; he would never let any of it go. One day Hot Suey ventured some advice to the Great Chan, "Because the people no longer have any gold to exchange for commodities or anything else, there are millions of people out of work and everybody is broke and many starving." He said, "The people need money to spend or all commerce will cease and the country will go broke."

"But the country is not broke," remarked the Great Chan smiling, "Just look at all the gold I have here in this room, and I am the country."

"Yes, yes, you are, oh Great One," Hot Suey replied, "but you are not the people, and the people languish and are starving. Commerce between them will soon cease. Eventually, you will have to use this gold to support them, if you do not give them some money to spend."

The Great Chan thought about this for days and finally called Hot Suey to his side and asked, "What is the cheapest thing we can use as money? I need to know because there are millions of people and if I must give them money I want to do it as cheaply as I can."

"Why little bits of paper are quite cheap, and you can make of them any amount of money you like, Oh Great One. We have many scribes that can print on the paper whatever denomination you wish."

"That is good," said the Great Chan, "but how do we know the people will accept these bits of paper as real money?"

Hot Suey asked for time to think on it. Within the week he reported back to the Great Chan. "Great Chan," he said, "I believe I have the answer to the problem of acceptance. Write upon each bit of paper money that it is real money and legal for all exchanges. You should also write upon it that the money is backed by not only the gold in the 'silver room' but the full faith and credit of the country's treasury and yourself. You can, if you wish, state that you back each yuan with a yuan's worth of gold; but have no fear. It does not mean that you will ever have to actually give up any of your gold, all you have to say is that the gold is backing up the paper. The people will be so glad to have money to spend that they will forget that it is just bits of paper and commerce will return, nobody will starve, and everyone will be happy as long as you keep your gold in your room. Beware of only one thing, my Great Lord, never let anyone in the country own any gold, because if you do, everyone will want some, and the paper will be used by the people to buy gold. Once this happens the value of the paper yuan will be set by how much gold it will buy and the paper will no longer have the value you write upon it."

"That seems easy enough," the Great Chan replied, "but it is hard to believe that my people are so gullible that they would actually believe that a small bit of paper would have the same value as gold. What makes you think they could be so stupid? Why, they would be satisfied by eating the menu instead of the dinner."

"Oh, Great One," Suey replied, "One must never underestimate the gullibility of the people. In the temples of religion the priests have been doing things like this for eons. When the people see that everyone else in the country accepts the law and each is placed under the same restrictions as his neighbor, they won't mind the restrictions at all. They will have no one to be jealous of. In a short time they will see that every one is spending these bits of paper and accepting these bits of paper just like they were gold, and the sheer number of transactions will convince everyone that the value of the paper is real. Why within a few months they will be hoarding this paper the same way they did the gold."

"This is fabulous!" shouted the Great Chan. "I must give you some gold for your sage advice."

"No, no, Great One, just give me a big pile of the printed papers. That will do the same thing for me. This will satisfy all my desires."

"Ho, Ho, Ho," laughed the Great Chan, "What a wonderful thing you have conceived, but how do we distribute the paper to the people properly?"

"We can go right back to the tax rolls and give the paper to the people we took the gold from. As long as we act fairly, the people will be happy," Hot Suey said.

"My dear Suey", the Great Chan replied, "You know we cannot be fair for long. It is not my nature nor anyone's to remain completely fair. What will happen when I decide to be unfair? I have many powerful friends and relatives to give favors to; I have generals and armies to support."

"I have figured that out too, all highest one", Hot Suey said, "It would not be wise to just give money to them. This would soon create jealously in the hearts of the people. It would be better to be in debt to these friends and simply pay interest on that debt annually. Then the people will believe that the recipients deserve your largess."

"Good!" said the Great Chan, "Let it be done and hurry. *Yet, what shall we call this paper that we distribute?*"

"We should call it 'cash'." Hot Suey said with a grin, "Cash will be seen as better than gold by the people because its value will be written on it, it will be easier to carry and exchange, and will never have to be weighed or measured or tested for purity. Cash will be 'king' for the people."

Hot Suey and the Great Chan began to laugh and laugh and

the Great Chan ordered a huge banquet with dancing girls. When he sat down to enjoy the feast, Hot Suey sat on the Chan's right side where he sampled all the fine delicacies of the kingdom.

It was done, and this was the invention of paper money. It worked just like it was supposed to and the people were happy, the Great Chan was happy and Hot Suey was happy too.

Many years passed, maybe a hundred and fifty, and Hot Suey and the Great Chan had been dead and buried for many years. The Great Chan number IV now ruled the Middle Kingdom, and one day he walked into the silver room and saw all the gold there. He did not care for gold like his great-grandfather. He liked cash and thought of it as "king" like the rest of the people, so he decided to sell the gold for cash and called on all the people to buy whatever gold they wanted from the silver room. He had a good heart and thought he was doing the people a favor.

Almost every family wanted to own some gold from the silver room as a keepsake to hand down from father to son, and so the people saved up their cash, until it seemed that every family in China bought gold from the silver room until all the gold was gone. The poor had bought a little and the rich a lot. They set it in special places in their houses or buried in their back yards for safekeeping. But at the end, when all the gold had been bought and stashed away by the people, large quantities of the cash circulating around the land had disappeared back into the government coffers. Now there was not enough cash for commerce and the people were becoming poor again because they would not sell their gold. The economy of the country collapsed and no one knew what to do about it. Since there were more people now than there had been a hundred and fifty years ago, and it took much more cash to buy one ounce of gold than it had before, there was soon no gold to back up the cash that was left in circulation. So the cash became almost as worthless as the paper it was written on. The people revolted and the Great Chan IV ran off to Japan, opened a Chinese restaurant, and the Middle Kingdom languished for centuries and centuries, right up to modern times.

The new government tried to retrieve the gold, but by now it was so well hidden around the country that it was impossible to find. Even some of the families that owned it forgot where it was hidden.

When the government tried printing more cash and distributing it to the people, the people no longer had much faith in the paper and spent it as fast as they could get it for any commodity available. Now the people were hoarding both gold and commodities and the country was really broke. It had no gold and no cash, just debts.

For our everlasting benefit an ancient historian recorded the history of this past period. He knew that if we could read about what happened long ago, we would never let it happen to us; and so we put our trust in well educated economists and bankers that study gold and money and cash, and we have lived happily ever after, I believe.

Miraculously, this entire subject was mentioned in one of Shakespeare's poems entitled, "A Pox upon This Blighted Land."

"A Pox upon This Blighted Land"

O' most worthy Chan, but man, proud man,
D'rest in a little brief authority, created money, tho most Ignorant of what he's most assured. This glassy essence, like an angry ape, plays such fantastic tricks before high heaven as makes sweet angels weep.

Now, all the world's a bank, and all the men and women merely Lenders and borrowers. They have their exits and entrances, and One man in his tyme plays many parts, but borrower most tymes.

So mighty Chan; we may pity though not pardon thee.
For now it so falls out that what we have we prize not to the Worth whilst we enjoy it, but being lacked and lost,
Why then we rack the value: then we find
The virtue that possession would not show us whilst it was ours.

Explain it out and leave not a stone upturned,

So that with monies let my knowledge come.
Now advance those great and weighty miens of four cornered
earth who know, who while their space and time at money's feet,
To sit and ponder, study and delve, distilling the drip of it.
I'm told and then . . .

Swift as a shadow, short as any dream,
Brief as the lightning in the collied night,
That in a spleen unfolds both heaven and earth,
And ere a man hath power to say "Behold!"
The jaws of darkness do devour it up!
How quick these bright things come to confusion.
Thus, we know them not, but only of results are seen.

So earth, man's once sweetly, warm abode, becomes a fool's
Paradise, And this, so strongly braced on paper and of gold,
Moved lurking men of money great, dark names, which
Truly thievery sought and power lustly gained, to
Bind up this earth in total sum with invisible
Cords of fiscal strength, unfathomed as Gordian's knot.
And stealthily as the viper stalks, like spider binds
Her prey with silent care, to feast upon our lives
Unto their quiet ends approach in times of spinner's
Leisure hours, as quiescence blooms in darkness,
When our heart grows cold and sickles over.

Why, they do bestride this narrow world like
A huge Colossus to the clouds; and we,
Petty men, slink about for crumbs and find
Ourselves dishonorable graves.
Men can be masters of their fates!
The fault, then does not lie in our stars,
But in ourselves, that all are underlings.
So Great Chan, Hot Suey and the rest,
Though ill-advised or greedy bent,
Should not be blamed for mankind's sorry
Plight into the deep and sinful night.

What is past is prologue: now we play our parts,
Skimming mother's milk and crushing men's hearts.
Thrusting, shoving, adulterating our brethren for but a shard
Of our sweet dreams of avarice and shame.
Cowards by stealth, Warriors by crime,
Cunning by guile, Loquacious by lies,
Honest by neglect, Stupid by sloth,
Undecided by inaction, Holy by hypocrisy.
On whom then hangs our fate?
Only the Jealous and Envious snap the bait.
On these weak reeds sole balance of world's case extends,
To temperate our wish't for ends.

Bottom Foam Beer

Augustus J. Schmaltzinger, a brewer for the now defunct Griesedeicke Brewery of St. Louis, experimented most of his lifetime looking for that "Holy Grail" of all brewmeisters, beer with the foam on the bottom. His method of experimentation was similar to that of his hero, the great Thomas Alva Edison: he would throw a handful of extraneous material into each new batch of mash and see what developed. One day in 1938 he was observed throwing a handful of goat liver pate into a new batch by Miss Gotcheye Moore, a bottle soaker who had recently been hired from the local Coca-Cola bottlers where she served as a coke sacker. Gotcheye reported Schmaltzinger's adultery to the media, so he resigned and moved to Milwaukee, where he reinstated his tried-and-true method of experimentation.

Augustus noted in early 1942 in his diary, after throwing a hand full of powdered uranium into a batch that the uranium bonded with the CO_2 in the foam. This caused the heavy substance UCO_2 (the foam, if you will) to fall to the bottom of each glass of beer drawn from this batch. After repeating the experiment successfully, he stripped naked and ran through the brewery shouting, "Eureka! Eureka!" until apprehended by a guard, arrested and sent to the big house for "philandering his mandamus" in public.

He returned to his position within a month of Sundays and

convinced the manager of the brewery that his brew would be a sensation. The experiment was done a third time with managers' approval. This experimental brew was tested by the finest beer brewers in Milwaukee, the ones that made the town famous for the beer it manufactured, and they found it to be a perfect mixture of taste, clarity, longevity, and advertising hoopla. As an added attraction, they also noted with extreme pleasure that this beer glowed in the dark, which had their advertising agency turning cartwheels of joy.

By this time, all the contracts for mass production of the beer had been signed, sealed and delivered. Schmaltzinger was made president of this new company, but the commodities administration of the U.S. Government had just declared uranium a class A war commodity, and the government refused all companies with German names access to uranium in any form.

Consequently, the new company shuttered its doors, and Schmaltzinger beer was never mass-produced. By the end of the war, the beer people felt that the "radioactive" beer might rightly, be perceived as a potential health hazard, and in spite of vehement protestations by Edward Teller, all plans to market the product were dropped.

Word of the new invention, however, had leaked to Walter Winchell in New York City in 1942 and inspired Dorothy Parker to write a powerful piece about this invention in her strong epic style. It will be repeated here in its entirety.

"Hamazing Brew"

It's here! Soon here!
That beer! Which beer?
The beer soon near.
It's all so clear.

So upside down,
Or right side up.
The foam is down.
The beer is up.

The beer that comes,
That we shall see,
Is rev el lou
Shun air er ee.

SHORT PEOPLE\ THE MORAL DILEMMA

(A DUAL TRILOGY PLUS ONE)

Individuals intent on exhibiting their poor taste have made sport and ridicule of short people. I feel these are stubby-sighted sadists with abbreviated attention spans and stunted IQs; they also have little self-esteem and tiny understandings. We should give them short or no shrift at all. Down through the millennia, many persons in authority, like Kings, Queens, and Jacks incited these practices. Though, somehow, no Aces got involved. Folk tales of pre-reformation Europe abound, branding the Popes and Monarchs of Germany and Eastern Europe with midgetry.

Throughout the ages these practices were reported as laced with sadism, masochism, coprophilia and sexual displays of a quite squalid nature, moving certain historians to the opinion that these intolerant, bigoted attitudes bordered on unfair bias. Now, in the near 21st century, however, no one remembers or cares, and many consider it all ancient history, which, coincidentally, it is. Still one should remember that Pygmy, Elf, Dwarf, Midget, Gnome and Troll have one thing in common: You're glad you're not one of them. Let's call a spade a spade. . . unless it's a sharpshooter.

A few tales of these unfortunate, or fortunate (depending on your particular point of view) creatures immediately follow this introduction. Some are well known to history and some not. However you view their moral dilemma is irrelevant, as each of these stories carries at the end a moral of its own that you can read. So you may suspend your moral deficiencies completely and find the sure, lasting and somewhat divine truth of the universal values inherent in "Life", as we know them. Without further ado I stand away from your path toward that "pot o' gold" at the end of the rainbow, and with a hearty "God speed" bid you on your merry way. Ta ta.

THE TIGER OF BORNEO

General Ito *"Squatty"* Sukahatchi was the smallest Japanese field commander in the Empire during World War II and he was appointed by the High Command, with a silent wink from Hirohito himself, to lead the invasion of Borneo in 1941. He was too short to actually land with his troops until 1942, as his feet were too small for the Navy's disembarkation ladders, and a special one had to be constructed for him out of seaweed. Immediately on landing, however, he briefed his troops who cheered him while discarding their long johns.

His plan of attack was a marvel of condensation, compression, and retrenchment, and using a short series of snubs, stunts, and shortcuts, nipped his enemy in the bud. They didn't call him the nippy little nipped-off Nip for nothing. He was a fearless leader and famous sexual deviant, unlike most famous Japs I know (none). Dr. Dick, also known as Richard Von Krafft-Ebing, believed the General was born tainted, but with what he never said. Squatty always questioned this diagnosis and mused he was a closet schmendrick. He tried to hide this taint from his men, afraid the knowledge could defile their defile, and he loved snappy parades. As the fighting reached a high pitch of excitement, he found it impossible to control himself, and immediately after the victorious engagement at Panalambadua (the original home of the famous *"wild man of Borneo"*), he ordered all the young native girls stripped and strapped to coconut trees. They were forced to run round and round these trees until they turned to butter, but after three days only two of them turned, and then only to margarine, so the experiment was canceled. This is how he got his name *"The Tiger."* Originally it was *"Tie Girl,"* but he shortened it; for phonetic purposes, I guess. The same way that the famous American singer Mel Torme changed his nickname from the *"Velvet-Frog"* to the *"Velvet-Fog."*

Ito's division became isolated as a result of McArthur's island hopping tactics. Forgotten until 1948, they nearly starved, before surrendering. In late 1949, Ito was accused of cannibalism by the National Enquirer and promptly set over for trial by a Japanese tribunal. Ito ably defended his innocence, proclaiming he only ate four soldiers and all of them had cloven hoofs but one who had a duckbill and tasted fowl (or foul). The prosecution proved a man wearing two army caps looked like a duck, and Ito admitted the resemblance was striking but reiterated he tasted fowl (bad?). Ito was exonerated but reprimanded to never do it again unless absolutely necessary.

He retired and traveled extensively. In 1960 he got lost in the monkey house at the San Diego Zoo and disappeared. Fifteen years later he was discovered on the outskirts of Phoenix anxiously licking discarded margarine pats from the dumpster of a short order cafe.

MORAL: *All bad mannered people do not have bad taste, but "people with bad taste" taste bad forever.*

FRENCH RESISTANCE FIGHTER

Guy Veaudeaux was a short French resistance fighter during World War II. His resistance fighting was short 'cause he was caught early by the Gestapo. He was short French, due to his poor grasp of vocabulary, and he was just plain short. The Gestapo tortured him by beating and kicking; bones were broken. Then they starved him for a week. . . no wine, French bread or béarnaise sauce with his filets. They stuck thin metal strips under his fingernails and heated them white hot with a torch until he sang the Marseillaise. He still would not talk. Next they hung him from a spinning ceiling fan by his feet for two days, which made him dizzy. He survived by fantasizing he was a partridge in a tornado, but sounded like a siren when he chirped. Still, he would not talk. Finally they tried psychological warfare on him for twenty-five minutes. He broke and turned in his innocent parents, wife and three kids. He just couldn't stand being called silly names.

During the trials at Nuremberg after the war, he turned up as a prison cook, until one day the M.P.'s caught him stuffing embarrassing notes into the prisoners' bratwurst. He is credited with causing Goering's suicide. Each night he'd sneak near the Field Marshal's cell and whisper over and over that Goering's face was covered with schmaltz. In 1955 he was discovered by a team of archaeologists in the castle ruins of the late Marquis de Sade, flapping his jack, and was forcefully hustled out of Provence. I last saw him at Cannes, where he was a part time film festival judge and local winery cork soaker. He was wearing a golden badge.

MORAL: *In France you may be a cork soaker and it's okay. But in the USA, it's demeaning to be a coke sacker, sock tucker, or the real McCoy.*

VIVA ZAPATA

Few Americans are privy to the truth behind the story of Emiliano Zapata, the heroic revolutionary leader of southern Mexico, but these days it is evident that Americans are not privy to most facts, having lost their privies during the great plumbing renaissance of the 1930's. The fact is he had a midget brother named *"Viva."* Viva was a dogged purveyor of revolution and revolting iguana tamales.

The famous Marlon Brando movie, conceived in Hollywood, would originally attempt to follow history closely, but Mickey Rooney, the first choice for Emiliano's brother, was lost on the MGM horror set *"Night of the Pee Pee's."* Anthony Quinn, the second choice, refused to play the part on his knees wearing big huaraches.

"They squeak too much." He beefed. Consequently, Quinn played the part at his full height, rumored to be five foot six. Thus, Hollywood felt unconstrained to shade historical facts in their production.

The facts are these. When Emiliano took over the government and became Presidente de Mexico, Viva demanded his famous brother make him five foot eight. Emiliano, faced with this most daunting task of his new office, discussed it at great length with cabinet leaders who agreed that Viva be laminated with prickly pear, then sprinkled with scorpions of his choice. Unfortunately prickly pear was out of season, and no choice scorpions could be found. He next discussed the problem with his trusted priest who suggested that Emiliano summarily declare Viva 5'8", and as long as he was at it he'd like to be Pope.

Emiliano ruminated and pondered, he worried and agonized; he knew he owed much to Viva who had been a heroic fighter for the revolution, and had saved his life on at least 68 separate occasions. He could never forget the last time when Viva, after an all night celebration, extracted a crazed guinea hen from his nose. Emiliano knew something must be done, but what and how? He prayed for insight, wisdom, understanding, intellectual power, sagacity, farsightedness, profundity and a new pair of boots. He walked stealthily downtown to the Cathedral to pray for guidance. There, alone, late at night, he heard a deep divine voice.

"It's all right, Emiliano." it said, "Grant your brother's wish; sign a proclamation that Viva is five-eight. Everything will be swell, but along with it, sign another, that each Mexican citizen is an additional foot taller. Then they won't be jealous of Viva. Trust me everything will be Jake."

"But, but," stammered Emiliano, "I don't know how to write, those quills keep breaking up."

"Quit worrying, Buster!" Replied the voice, "When you leave the Cathedral you will find a present from me behind the font."

The voice trailed away into silence and Emiliano, hoping for his new boots, headed directly for the font near the door. There, he only found a box of used crayolas, but used them to sign the two proclamations the next morning. They were nailed to Cathedral doors around the nation. At first the peons rejoiced, but later they realized they would all need new clothes to fit their taller frames, then the tailors rejoiced. Now they were too tall for their beds. The furniture makers rejoiced. They now had to stoop to enter the doors of their houses, the adobe masons rejoiced. Rejoicing was pervasive, even among the conservatives, who only joiced, until they suddenly realized that the pretty, exotic, sweet women of Mexico, their wives and girl friends were much too tall. They still wanted to woo those petite five-foot-two brown beauties, but now none could be found. They set up such a hue and cry as had never been heard around the land, for the natives rarely hued. Emiliano was heartbroken. He decided to leave the presidential palaces and return to the southern Mexico countryside. He abandoned government, and late one night stole out of Mexico City never to return. His second proclamation was ripped and torn off every Cathedral door in the land, but the first, proclaiming Viva Zapata five-foot-eight, remained.

Many years have passed, since Emiliano sat behind the presidential desk in the seat of power of the Mexican nation. Now, people have long forgotten his first name, but the popular *"Viva Zapata"* posted on the Cathedral doors for many years, still remains the legacy of this great man of conscience.

P.S. The origin of the mysterious voice in the Cathedral has never been uncovered, although the janitor remembered a large pile of red tipped cigarette butts and chicken feathers behind the nave.

Editor's Note. *General Huerta, Zapata's enemy, was an inveterate chain smoker who preferred red tipped cigarettes. He was also known to be fond of eating chicken and, earlier in his youth, was the resident geek for the Barnum and Bailey circus in the southern USA. On his deathbed he still spoke geek fluently.*

MORAL: **Beware of geeks bearing gifts, especially in Mexico City.**

THE DEAD SEA TROLLS

During one of my many visits to foreign climes, I chanced upon a Bedouin tribesman hustling Arabian mocha in a Jericho bar and grill. Rarely, had I seen such haunted eyes outside of cold-fusion laboratories. When he served my coffee, thick with rancid olive oil and sugar, I, sensing a story, grabbed his sleeve which immediately unraveled in my grasp, revealing a series of branded chicken faces and swastikas all up and down his arm. I was shocked into mock silence and saw a mocking expression on his pockmarked face that resembled a French coq clock I had once stroked.

"Arrha vish! Enfeendi!" He screamed, masterfully disguising his lethargy, while attempting to hide his arm from view by rubbing it vigorously with his other hand from wrist to shoulder. Desiring to know more, I tossed him a shekel or two and bade

him sit, which to my surprise, he did almost quickly, having never been bade before. He could not speak English or I Arabic so we tried broken French pidgin until the table and floor became littered with the feathers. We conversed furtively for two hours or until my fistula began to throb, whichever was more. He told me an amazing tale, which I will now relate to you or your relatives, whichever is relevant, and in your native tongue, but if you have no native tongue, a pound of sliced salami will do.

"I had been fishing on the West Bank of the Dead Sea all morning without any luck, and when the temperature approached 140 degrees, I decided to climb a nearby hill and look for a cool nook, or some nookie or both. Fortunately, I found a small cool opening in the rocks just large enough to squeeze my head into, so I removed my turban and stuck it in (My head not my turban, Dum Dum!). I dozed for a time but was suddenly awakened by the sound of martial music and crowds of small foreign voices shouting 'Deutschland Uber Alles!' I opened my eyes and could barely make out a small band of trolls dressed in shorts with broad suspenders and Tyrolean hats. They were goose-stepping and strutting around churlishly; stomping their little jackboots, flailing about and screaming obscenities at each other, flaunting their bananas and truncheons.

"'Aha! Australians,' I guessed. They rapidly formed into a flying wedge and suddenly rushed my head. Before I could move, two jumped onto my nose, another in one ear and three began pulling on my lips. I heard one barking out orders, and they released a sweet acrid gas into my nostrils that I believe was lilac, edelweiss or Xyclon B. I awoke after midnight with a sore arm, a headache and a small troll-scroll under my tongue which read, 'Free schnapps at the Tiergarten, June 9, 1943', but it was already 1951. I thought, 'Oh mighty Allah, are you playing another trick on me?'

"Weeks later I sent the troll scroll to the Tiergarten, Newark, New Jersey but only received one hot bottle of beer by return mail."

His story thus ended on a low note, B-flat, I believe, so using his directions and wearing my best plug hat, I searched the same hills near the Dead Sea for over two weeks, trying to rediscover the trolls but to no avail.

I found a small replica of the Siegfried line flying little white flags but no more scrolls, so I resigned myself to buy my own beer.

MORAL: *In these days nothing is dependable, not even the Dead Sea Trolls.*

THE GNOMES OF ZURICH

Sitting, having a drink at a sidewalk cafe in Geneva in 1954, I found myself lost in conversation with a small stocky man. He wore a bright horizontally striped polo shirt and beret, and was trying to peddle fine Swiss watches from his arm. However, when he saw my stainless Timex, complete with a khaki band, he knew it would be easier to pedal a bicycle up the Alps then to sell an expensive watch to an American of such immaculately ascetic taste. I told him I was a writer of tales and other BS and asked if he was a Nazi, a midget, or anything newsworthy like that? He shook his little, rotund, fat head sadly and with just a hint of hubris said, "No, I'm chust und gnome from Zurich."

Well, I'd heard from Ike about these Zurich gnomes before. They were related to the Egyptians or gypsies for short, and he was plenty short. I offered him a drink of Kir and asked to hear his story for the folks back home in Texas.

"Oh, Tex-asss!" the little moon face said, his dark, beady, little eyes arching wide and round while a pig smile spread slowly across his face. Then he turned his head and spat disgustedly on the sidewalk by my left penny loafer, possibly mimicking those old tobacco chewers in the westerns.

"Mine name iss Sotheby Bugeroni, und mine forefadder Stifter migrate to Zurich in zee 16th zentury mit dee Moldavian crown jewels. Hiking toward Zurich he meets hiss gousin Spaniel Polax from Croatia, who goincidentally had stole zat gountry's crown jewels; und mit yedelgetter dey make und long trek across zee Alps to Zurich."

"Hang on a gol danged minute, Sotheby, are you sure people knew how to ride hosses in Europe in the 16th century?" I asked, trying to keep him on his toes.

"Hawzis? Hawzis? I don't know from Hawzis!" He screamed back, spittle oozing from the corners of his lips and his nose running, "Zey ver valking! It vast und perilous und cold chourny, but finally zee pair arrive mit Shiksa Pass vhere zay make pass at zome young shiksas, und, I'm told zee girls make zem werry happy gnomes. Vhen dey arrived mit Zurich, dey zell zee jewels to some Hapsbirds and found zee First International Gnome Bank und Bakery.

"Zee business prosper for zenturies until Vorld Var II. Den tings really pick up. Gelt flows in from all over Europe. Everybody opens massive zecret accounts. Vee charge zem for safe keeping und give mit zem free rolls ven zay ver in town. Nein utter bank can bake like us, Nein!"

"Yawl mean to tell me there are nine bank and bakery combinations in Zurich, Sotheby? I'd say you are beginning to stretch things a bit my boy. If you want me to report your story back in Texas you alls gonna have to stick to the truth." I said, using my best J. Edgar Hoover impersonation; tapping my index finger hard on the glossy table top while frowning and squinting menacingly into his good eye.

"Nein, No, No nine, Nien; ve haff ze only von, zee only combo in town. Himmler ankommen often. He vass und zucker for zee pies, und gonsidered himself und real pie gonnoisseur. He vould alvays eat zem from zee inside out, but gouldn't tell currants from raisins. Vhen it came to goose-stepping though, he vass first glass. I svear both hiss veet vould be in zee hair at vonce. Vee became great friends. He vonce told me, how before de var, he liffed in a cave mit only hiss pet donut he called Inge. Vhat a guy! Den von day in 1942 Himmler goose-stepped in to open more accounts ein started eating custard pie, vehn I noticed ein beautiful diamond encrusted voman's vatch on hiss arm mit ein broken glasp secured mit ein rubber band. I immediately recognized it ass belonging to mine famous maiden aunt, Her Grand Gnomness uff Bratislovia. I had heard rumors uff zee goncentration camps und vass infuriated, zhinking how he'd stolen mine poor aunt's vatch. I determined to act und act now, so I inwite him back into zee waults to vitness zee opening uff ein case uff gefilte fish recently gonfiscated from zee Varsaw ghetto. He gouldn't resist. Und on zee vay back I deftly bit through zee gamey rubber band und jokingly told him how gut it veals to shtick ein arm undo zee wacuum tubes dat vee use to movff paper around zee bank. He gouldn't vait, und vhen vee got to zee row uff tubes in zee wault, he schtuck hiss arm in to feel zee bleasant wacuum. I haff him keep it in a few minutes so he vould experience zee tingling zensation. Vehn he pulled it out, he neffer noticed mine aunt's vatch vass gone. Heh, heh, he zinks it feels gut, und giggling, asks if he can be left alone viss zem for a vile, but I explain it vass against bank bolicy. Vehn vee oopened zee cases in zee wault vee find zey vass stuffed mit latkes und zere vas only ein jar uff gefilte fish. Himmler vass infuriated vhen I ate more zen mine share and had me kicked out of zee bank. Mine fadduh vould not let me back in vhen he discovered I'd let a Nazi play mit hiss wacuum. He'd always gonsidered it his own zecret. So now I zell vatches on zee street in Geneva."

Before we parted, I told him to look me up when he came to America. He said he would but never wanted to actually stay and get neutralized. To this day he's only dropped into the ranch twice on weekends, and never told me what happened to his aunt's watch. I'd tell you his hobby, but you'd never eat seafood again. That's a gnome for you.

MORAL: *A tricky gnome like a sticky wicket is bad news in peace or war.*

THE O'GALVIE'

Tromp, Trump, Tromp
The Floys are blushing,
Whenever will the chicken seeds run dry?
Stomp, Stamp, Stomp
Old Shaw is gushing,
With ringlets floating to the sky.

Macgillacuddy's song is fleeting,
While spanning Chloe flaunts his jack.
Dobbs and Spots are flipping,
With leprechauns snapping at their flak.

Blap, Bip, Blap,
The beards are foaming
When the twilight of the morning meets the day.
Flip, Flop, Flip,
The cloys are growing.
Can ever it be far to Maculay?

Macgillacuddy's song is fleeting,
While spanning Chloe flaunts his jack.
Dobbs and Spots are flipping,
With leprechauns snapping at their flak.

The enigmatic lines of the *"O'Galvie'"* reverberated between my ears as I boarded the night train from Dublin to Maculay and points west by southwest, deep into the untamed hinterlands of Ireland. I'd been commissioned by the Old Bushmill chapter of the Saint Patrick's Day Parade and Shit-faced Society to make this trip, try to uncover O'Galvie's meaning and grab a leprechaun to smuggle out of Eire for next year's parade.

The members had been convinced that Maculay was the place to accomplish all this as the O'Galvie' had been poured over by some of the finest Irish alcoholic spirits old Houston ever produced. Sure the O'Galvie' was considered one of the most explicitly obtuse poems O'Connor had ever written, but the vote was near unanimous and who was I to disagree. My own knowledge of the "Emerald Isle" was next to nothing. However, being fortified by the overwhelming vote, and a couple stiff shots, I agreed in my precise, rather literal, and quite austere manner to lift the banner of duty to its penultimate and do my best to further those plans of mice and men that *"gang aft agley."* (Scots-Irish?)

A few weeks later (though hardly lost), I found myself sitting in a cramped compartment of the dingy green foreigner's car reading a small yellow pamphlet entitled, Tips to Non-Irish Travelers. Among the lists of currency exchanges, weights, measures and etcetera, I noticed the explicit instruction, "Wave and be sure to have your head out the window when arriving at your destination. This happy greeting," it said, *"will stamp you as an honored guest, since few foreigners travel near the southwest coast of this land."*

'Twas a bit past midnight when the old rickety train moved jerkingly, slowly decelerating into the Maculay station. A few other outsiders and I were partially hanging out of the windows, waving, smiling, and greeting the natives. They rushed to the train before it had fully stopped, pulled us off through the windows and beat us to a pulp with strange knobby cudgels and shillelaghs. Unconsciousness rapidly descended on my broken frame, yet, I remembered thanking God for the gift before I passed out.

When I awoke, I was being dragged trophy-like to the local pub, where their drinking continued and mine commenced. Swilling mugs of warm Irish whiskey was a real treat, as I discussed the O'Galvie' with a number of ancient, bearded alcoholics, who seemed intent on deep frying my suitcase, while revealing the poem's shadowy mysteries. For example, Macgillacuddy and Chloe were, they said, legendary lovers of Bunyonesque proportions, and crude replicas of certain of their body parts were engraved on rest room walls throughout the city. They gave the phrase *"getting your Irish up"* new meaning. O'Connor used chicken seeds to refer, Aggie-Iike, to eggs he prepared for the planting season. I was assured that *"Old Shaw"* was a warm spring whose misty ringlets do seem to float heavenward on each night of the new moon, and have done so as far back as their collective memories go, estimated at about 3 years. The *"Floys"* are a type of pale lavender wild flower that appear to blush when covered with either Irish dew or red paint; I was never sure which. Finally Dobbs and Spots is the name of an ancient cobbler house where you can get your shoes half-soled while still wearing them.

Now to one familiar with the *"O'Galvie'"*, and you should be one by now, having already read this far. You must know that Dobbs and Spots are the pair intimately associated with the prime objective of my search. I then and there determined, when morning rolled around, to make a quiet visit to this shop of renown, and see if I might cozy up a bit to my quarry.

"When the twilight of the morning reached the day" we were unceremoniously swept out of the pub into the street. My mind reeling from the booze; I crawled around a lot looking for lodgings. Although, I expected no quarter in my quixotic quest among these quenchless, quarrelsome, quibbling and quirky queers. This quandary quelled my quavers, qualms and quakes. Quizzically I quailed at quaffing a quart of a quaggy, squid-like, alcoholic quagmire costing only a quid. I was queasy and quasi-nauseated. Quaint? I questioned quietly. Quit? I queried quickly. No! Just drunk again! Quiescence quilted my senses.

I awoke around noon in jail where I'd been charged with flailing without a license. I paid my fine, no lo contendere, and stole both out of the courtroom, and the judge's thermos. Walking down the main street, it was easy to find Dobb's and Spot's Shoe Hospital and Diagnostic Clinic. It was housed in an archaic, three-story, stone building and sported a hanging wooden sign depicting a large black high top shoe in bed with a thermometer under its pale tongue. I ventured in. What a startling sight met my eyes? There were large revolving wheels and drums connected by leather belts of all lengths and widths from floor to ceiling, across the ceilings, across the floors, turning other wheels and gears in a wonderfully moving complexity that would have been a nineteenth century engineer's dream. Though, sadly I recalled that all nineteenth century engineers were now extinct, except maybe in Russia and places like that. The incessant hum of the machinery brought tears to my eyes as its steady beat reminded me of my last night in a disco bar.

I approached a short, rubicund man who turned out to be rather garrulous, I believe, and I finally struck a deal with him (though he struck me first) for a half-sole job, but only after agreeing to let him garnishee my wages for the next three years. Dobbs and Spots, together and separately, wrapped me in some large furniture pads and strapped me within the loops of two pristinely filthy leather belts that hung from the ceiling. I was hoisted some meter or so off the ground. I was not exactly sure about the meter 'cause I can't sing a note.

I felt myself rotating slowly, as the work began. This was not unpleasant, as I am used to feeling myself. It was possible now to observe all the nooks and crannies in the place, as I rotated slowly with an occasional flip. The baseboard seams, around the tables and floors, the inaccessible cracks in the walls and the ceiling rifts all fell in the way of my rotating gaze. Suddenly, I noticed movement! Of what, I was still unsure. It was rapid and seemed to disturb a luminescent dust that sparkled in the sunlight beams haphazardly shining through the roof. I noticed movement in the cracks and crevices of the walls, ceilings, and floors. Soon, by concentrated effort, I could discern the rapid motion of very small, glowing, live bodies that disturbed this dust, but whether caused by leprechauns or insects was as yet unclear. I was just in process of focusing my eyes on one of these streaking bodies when I felt a shoe nail being driven into my big toe. Before I could scream, I heard some Irish curses to St. John the bastard and felt it extracted.

Dobbs, the rubicund one, laughed, and said that by virtue of the lucky nail I had won the use of a famous Dobbs and Spots crooked walking stick, which I could use freely as long as I was within the building. I was momentarily overcome, as this was the first thing I'd ever won without cheating.

The half sole-job done, I hobbled up to the counter and asked Dobbs if leprechauns caused the movements I had seen, but he just crooked his big forefinger around his nose with a wink and shortchanged me.

Later I approached Spots, the introverted one of the pair. I felt sure he was introverted 'cause he wore two pair of pants with the zipper in back, and when I asked about the leprechauns he fell down! I persisted until he promised to meet me on the outskirts of town near the Cloy dell after dark. Cloys, I discovered, are reddish, floppy mushrooms that raw, taste like radishes, but when cooked, the taste magically changes into three day old oatmeal. We met, and Spots, after my promises to never tell and send him a Kennedy Half Dollar, admitted that the *"wee people"*, as they are called, are all really big roaches.

"'Tis true they clean up wee bits o'food that's left around. He said. *"But they ne'er pay their share o'rent. Still,"* he declared, in his broken, quaint English, *"'tis a foiner name, as roaches cast a moir ruined milieu and completely peg out the ambiance of our green Isle."*

I arrived back in Houston just in time to report to the society and explain certain meanings of the O'Galvie' to the astonished group. When they asked about the leprechauns, I said I had seen them but didn't believe in *"bringing coals to Newcastle."* They seemed confused and disgruntled for awhile until the booze was served.

MORAL: **Remember, when dealing with the Irish, their morals maybe too pungent for eloquence.**

ARACHIBUTYROPHOBIA (A WHIMSY)
(THE FEAR OF PEANUT BUTTER STICKING TO THE ROOF OF THE MOUTH)

Woody Allen was a short comedy writer and part-time movie star who wrote extensively in comedic circles but he longed to write in squares. Try as he might, it eluded him. Possibly because as a child he suffered from arachibutyrophobia and this malady followed him into adulthood and hooded his adolescence too. Consequently, he couldn't eat the famous peanut butter stew so popular in square circles, which, I understand, are the largest circles in the U. and S. A.

Poor Woody seemed destined to remain in minority circles,

those circuitous ones of rounded hyperbole. This made him sad, but then he was sad anyway and never seemed to realize that the sad was funny and the funny was sad. One day he grew overtired of being sad. He sat in the sand and cursed the sad, saying "Sad damn! Sad damn!" Others, misunderstanding, picked up the chant, and "Saddam! Saddam!" became so popular that Saddam was on the front pages of all the newspapers and his picture on all the TV sets and he became the most well known man in the world. He was quite happy with his new found popularity till one day the UN sent a shipment of brown stuff in jars for the children of his land. Saddam thought it was quite a mean thing to send crunchy camel dung to the children of his country so he got exercised and began exercising until he wore himself out trying to exorcise the UN The people of the world started laughing at him and one day shortly afterward he tasted it. To his dismay he found he had arachibutyrophobia too. This made him despondent, which led to sadness. Unfortunately, it was too late, and the world now laughed at both Woody and Saddam and neither could do anything to stop it.

MORAL: *Regardless of one's motive, laughter and sadness go hand in hand and nobody really appreciates people not in square circles. Especially, if they have arachibutyrophobia.*

TRUTH STRANGER OR FICTION?

INTRODUCTION

Someone once said, "Truth is stranger than fiction," but the insidious fact is, he was a <u>stranger</u>. Could this conspiracy have been planned, or was it just a chain of fortuitous circumstances? The statement, nevertheless, has been repeated so often it has become part of our common vernacular, whatever that is. But is it <u>truth</u>? Who knows? Who cares? <u>You do</u>! Like any literate person of intelligence you are a <u>seeker of the truth</u>. It is inborn in you, whether you admit it or not, and manifests itself every time you search for your keys. I have cleverly devised and/or blundered onto a method or game designed to test your ability to differentiate between truth and fiction. You may, however, be at a disadvantage if you've never studied differentials at all (like differential calculus, differential equations, or automobile differentials), then again maybe not.

The history stories that follow, which I have deftly composed, are crammed with both truth and fiction. They enable you of <u>intelligence,</u> a democratically achieved trait, to discern between the two. You should have no major problems, but do not be too hasty in your judgements, or you might find yourself taken in by the truth and be embarrassed. This may not be the first time, as those of you with weak bladders, having previously embarrassed yourself, during your own personal "moments of truth," already know.

Of course, the actual conversations portrayed are normally considered as fiction out of hand, due to the dearth of hand-held recorders available to historians prior to the late twentieth century. Still, should historical sources be found that mimic the portrayed conversations, within the rhetorical bounds of fact, the words must be considered as truthful as those accepted within courts of American jurisprudence, as imprudent as that is. But let's not split hairs when there are too many around already, especially in people's ears. Just be sure to check your answers either in the Encyclopedia Britannica or the history books of your choice. If you're still not sure, or are too lazy to check, just write me for the reference. That might work, though probably not.

In order to get you into the correct mental mood for the task ahead, I'll pose a few statements with clues designed to condition you to the constant, variable mind-set necessary for a first rate intellectual, like you, to achieve a successful result.

Truth or Fiction: (pick only one)

1. *Some egg whites are black, but no egg blacks are white.*
   Clue: Ignore the racial overtones.

2. *Certain Hollywood movie stars have been reported to use chicken fat as an aphrodisiac while at prayer.*
   Clue: Geeks do not live by bread alone.

3. *A famous mathematician-physicist was a well known sexual exhibitionist.*
   Clue: Great men may do great things alone in the bathroom.

4. *A great philosopher believed he had more than two monads.*
   Clue: Individuals believing they have less than two are exempt.

5. *Archaeologists have discovered that frottage was first performed to exhaustion by a tribe of ancient Frenchmen in the Roquefort District of France.*
   Clue: Some cheeses simply cannot be ignored.

6. *Certain flamboyant monarchs of well-known European countries suffered from amnesia, nesia, pregenital fixations, and plain old pregenitals.*
   Clue: Pick one!

7. *Mary Queen of Scots gave Scotophilia its bad name.*
   Clue: "Haggis" may sound bad, but "eating it" is worse.

8. *The term voyeurism was coined from a particular voyage of Ulysses, but the coin had little value.*
   Clue: I'll grant that this was not the Civil War!

From the above sample historical oddities it is clear to see that the line between truth and fiction is a flimsey one at best; as is a general knowledge of history. Now please go on with the stories, and don't worry, I'm sure you will do admirably.

OUR AEGEAN CHRYSALIS (APOLOGIES TO DURANT)

The search for the distinction between <u>noumenon</u> and <u>phenomenon</u>, between the unseen real and the unreal seen, burst upon the western world stage right after its construction in the ancient Greece of the 5th century B.C., and brother, that puts us on a very slippery, old and rancid slope. The philosophical battle between idealism and materialism, which then began, has continued intermittently to the present day. Casualties of the battle, however, have remained relatively light, except for a long recess during the Dark Ages when everybody agreed on *"burning at the stake"* to settle their philosophic differences. Thus, the search of men for a moral basis of life, man's way of existence in it, and why, has been the goal of western philosophy ever since the pyramid construction market crashed in 500 B.C.

How did it all come about? Why did these ancient Greeks invest such time and effort to discover the answers? Has this had any effect on modern man, and why not? Who cares? Definitely not I! Yet on the other hand, who among you is so base as to disown your own heritage? Who among you is so crass not to expend a bit of time to find the truth? Who among you is so profane not to march to the beat of your personal drummer? On second thought, don't answer that!

First, we'll set the stage with a quick glance at the religion of that day. The theology of the Grecian Gods had no relationship with any moral code. In fact the Gods consisted of rapists, thieves, liars, deviants, procrastinators, murderers, torturers, beasts, arsonists, adulterers, cowards, pillagers, and then you had the really bad guys. It was in this time that <u>Pheidias</u>, a florid, religious zealot, exhorted the Greeks to ennoble their Gods with beauty, majesty, fine heroic statuary and other works of art, and this stirred <u>Xenophanes</u>, a soft spoken, modest, introverted writer and philosopher; the author of the popular work *"How to Tie*

Your Shoes," to declare *the Gods were myths.* These words electrified the countryside and upset many pious Greeks, Greek Gods, and a few myths and mythters. They outlawed his books, and placed a curse on his head which he was forced to wear both indoors, and out. It was not too gauche but needed blocking every two weeks.

Thus, speaking one's mind in Ancient Greece, even before Christianity was invented, was a tricky business fraught with peril, and yet, in this seething caldron of ferment, great minds began to stir the towns and fertile countryside with portentous discoveries, new ideas and a few bags of kitty litter.

Pythagoras, of the famous theorem, became so taken with the perfection of the right triangle that he associated his geometry-mathematics with philosophy and religion. He believed the support of immortality would stimulate morals, especially if one could create one's own 90 degree angle. However, he suffered from disgustingly poor taste and was never able to differentiate between good and bad morals. *"We need morals,"* he said, *"good or bad, we just need more morals."*

Protagoras doubted, Socrates ignored, Democritus denied, and Euripides ridiculed his stance on this, but all of their protractors were faulty.

The Idealists

Parmenides was annoyed by Xenophanes, or the Xylophone (it's not clear which), and he declared *"All things are one and never change,"* but he was single and only had one pair of sheets. *"Not being cannot be,"* he declared cautiously, having never watched George Raft perform, and added, *"There is no void,"* but this was rarely accepted and finally disproved after Nixon's cranial x-rays were made public. To cap his illustrative career he declared that motion was unreal; *"It assumes,"* he said, *"the passage of something from where it is to where there is nothing but empty space, and since not being cannot be, there cannot be empty space."*

Zeno was aghast at this denial of motion and tried to disprove it for over three hours. Finding this impossible, he changed his mind and offered many logical proofs of Parmenides' motionless world.

94

"If a body tried to move from point A to point B," he reasoned, *"it would have to arrive at midpoint C first, but in order to do this, would have to arrive at midpoint D between A and C and so on ad infinitum. As there are an infinite number of midpoints, it would never actually have time to get to B no matter how fast it was traveling. Thus, though our senses detect motion, it is in actuality metaphysically unreal."* He was hailed by many of the intellectials as one of the greatest philosophers of his day, until he was arrested, tortured and then accidentally killed by an apparently moving meat-axe splitting his skull by mistake. It was thrown at a wall that he was midway from. For his efforts, <u>Zeno</u> became known as the father of logic, and the patron saint of all parked cars.

<u>Erechtheus</u> was one of the first materialists. He was exceptionally well endowed and went to great lengths to prove that motion did in fact exist. It is said he brought tears to the eyes of many of his female assistants while performing his proofs in front of large audiences of students and detractors. Many women worshiped him as a God, and he operated a successful asylum in Athens devoted to the intensely self-deprecated. When he personally treated them *"Greek Fashion"* the strident cries, *"I am sombody!"* could be heard for blocks around (though most were square).

Parenthetically, it must be added that an equally sucessful antithetical asylum was opened across town from which could be heard the cries: *"I am nobody!"* and *"Where is the meat?"*

Greece was a very superstitious country in those days. Before going out of the house a man would pat himself on the head, both shoulders and hips, on each of his knees and the bottoms of his shoes. He would kiss the door and each of the abode's occupants, never forgetting to tap his feet three times on the threshold while gently squeezing his private parts with both hands, if possible. Sometimes this had to be done quickly as this was before windows and many had to rush outside to breathe. He would wash his hands, sprinkle himself at the *"Nine Springs,"* and put a bit of bay leaf from the Temple into his mouth. Once outside, if a cat crossed his path, he would continue no farther until he threw three rocks across the street. If he spied a urinating dog, he would quickly avert his eyes lest he turn into stone, and this was considered a distinct possibility, especially if the dog carried his own Medusa. If he saw a snake he would take the day off and build a shrine to Dionysus on the spot. Should a Greek pass a smooth stone at a crossroads, he would anoint it with oil, kneel down, and worship it for a while.

Spitting on oneself was the best known toxin for warding off evil spirits; it was done with gusto and in multiples should an epileptic, madman or two-headed person come into view. If any of the above exhibited deviant behavior, spitting was inadequate, and the viewer would make a concerted attempt to retch up his breakfast of figs, porridge and olive oil. A sneeze, hiccup, stumble or cough was a sufficient evil portent to cancel any planned trip. The Spartans claimed their leader stumbled on a small pile of lentils, and had to cancel their march to Marathon to relieve the apparently doomed Greek defenders there. In spite of the great victory, the Spartans took it philosophically.

The Materialists

The famous <u>Leucippus</u> studied under <u>Zeno</u>, and while attempting to demonstrate his newly invented one man seesaw, fell and fractured his skull. It was during his three-year convalescence that he developed his famous notion of a void and used it to prove that motion did in fact exist. He polished up his statement which came to be known as the *"<u>Leucippus Imperative</u>"* and follows: *"The universe contains only atoms and space and nothing else. These atoms must coalesce and fall together to create the planets, pots, pans, plates, and everything else that starts with a 'P'."* This precise, perceptive, and persuasive dictum undercut <u>Zeno's</u> anti-motion logic completely and <u>Zeno</u> gave up philosophy and became a wrestling teacher. <u>Leucippus</u> was the picture of health for years until his head, aimlessly, rotted off.

<u>Socrates</u> also ridiculed <u>Zeno's</u> logic and dialectical method, but he secretly must have liked it a lot, because he used it in his haughty manner, while petulantly strutting around Athens for years, confounding its citizens with weird metaphysical questions, like *"would you rather eat a dozen rotten oysters or defecate in your hose?"* When he would finally coax an answer

from the puzzled passers-by, he would chuckle at them and say, *"Why did you pick that one? You must be crazy!"* Then he'd start laughing at them. After the citizens took almost all of this they could stand, they had him bollixed. Since there was always a question of his piety, and he never wrote anything, certain conservatives of today believe that <u>Socrates</u> was a ficticious character whom <u>Plato</u> invented as a character in his books about Socrates. These people still believe that John Wayne was America's greatest hero.

We next come to <u>Democritus</u>. This callous, indolent youth came from a rich family, and spent his early years traveling only to settle down later in Athens. He then proceeded to lethargicaly publish a few papers on math, physics, astronomy, navigation, geography, anatomy, physiology, psychology, music, psychotherapy, medicine, philosophy, art and erotic bowel movements. He had studied music in Thebes with <u>Philolaus</u>, who, having never heard modern rock and roll, believed that everything musically takes place by necessity and in harmony. <u>Democritus</u> applied this notion to the universe and agreeing with <u>Leucippus</u>, thought that everything consisted of only atoms and the void.

He lost his money and clothes to crooked gamblers one night and a week later wrote, *"There is no chance,"* and believed chance to be a fiction invented to disguise ignorance. He was the first to say that matter can neither be created nor destroyed. *"Only forms change."* He wrote, after watching a runaway pastry cart crush the famous marble statue of Aphrodite at Corinth. He added, *"Even my change changes,"* after being short-changed at a fig stand. <u>Democritus</u> lived to well over 100 years and when very old said, *"Happiness is fitful and sensual pleasure brief satisfaction; it doesn't get harder as you get older, just fat. The wise should cultivate happiness within himself, 'specially when no one else is around."* He attempted suicide by starving himself, but he loved honey and continued to smell it. He began stuffing it up his nose and ultimately sweetened himself to death.

<u>Empedocles</u> was a master of rhetoric and was more of a mystic than the other philosophers of his day. He was neither

idealist nor materialist. Famous for saying, *"Idealism offends the senses and explains all but the world, while materialism offends the soul and explains all but life,"* he believed that love and hate, good and evil, left and right and wrong fight and balance each other in the vast universal rhythm of life and death. Many credit him as the first *"evolutionist"* and say he declared that all higher forms of life develop from lower forms, (though they admit he thought himself a God and his kids a passel of idiots). Empedocles coined the phrase, *"Everything is made of earth, air, fire, and water,"* and afterward decided to become a vegetarian. He curiously called fools, *"Vain fools,"* and vain fools, *"Fools,"* enhancing his mystic reputation. At one of his stand-up lectures he said, *"For that what is, no eye has seen, no ear has heard, nor can it be conceived by the mind of man. Now see! Did you hear what I said, and do you understand?"* Later he brought a dead woman back to life and disappeared with her into a cave.

Protagoras, the Sophist, which is roughly equivalent to a college professor, accepted sensation as the only means to knowledge and refused to admit to any transcendental reality, except for his high teaching fees. *"There is no absolute truth,"* he said, *"but only such truths as hold for some under certain conditions; contradictory assertions can be equally true for different people or at different times,"* but he only truly believed this after a big breakfast of bacon and eggs. *"All subjective things are relative,"* he said, *"but my relatives are not subject to this."* He portrays man as the sole arbiter of all things; *". . . of those that are, that they are, and of those that are not, that they are not."* Today, Protagoras is considered individualism's first great voice and the forerunner of rock concerts, boom boxes and irritating teenagers. A blow to educated people everywhere, his philosophy disposes all of us, regardless of our ignorance, to consider ourselves proper judges of the moral code; free to rationalize our desires and reject anything we don't understand or approve of, like owning six cats or eating sour pickles and ice cream. Protagoras is credited as the philosophical inspiration for Descartes' famous expression, *"Good sense is, of all things among men, the most equally distributed; for everyone thinks himself so abundantly provided with it that . . . they do not desire a larger measure than they already possess."* This has later been attributed variously to Mark Twain, Yogi Berra and me.

Protagoras was an agnostic and said he didn't know what the Gods were like or if they existed. *"Many things prevent our knowing,"* he added, *"the subject is obscure and brief our life."* The Athenians, on hearing this insult to their beliefs, ran him out of town and he drowned, justifying his brief life prognostication in spades. That's Athenians for you, pious to a fault yet not trivial.

Gorgias of Thebes was another agnostic, but since he didn't live in Athens, figured he could say what he liked and get away with it. He wrote, *"Nothing other than the senses exist and if anything else existed it would be unknowable, and if it were knowable, it could not be communicated from one person to another."* Although the people of Thebes knew he was an agnostic, they misspelled it and thought it described a person that doubted the existence of eggs. Thus, Gorgias lived over a hundred years. He was still playing a fair game of one-legged sphairistai (Greek handball) until ironically, one day in his nineties, after missing three serves in a row, the spectators egged him beyond all recognition.

Moving quickly now to the fourth century B.C., we glimpse a new liberated breed of scientist-mathematicians and philosophers, most of whom came out of the Socratic School in Athens or were tutored by a person who did. You may recall that Socrates claimed he knew nothing but the right questions to ask. These guys knew all the answers, but they forgot the questions.

The Scientist-Mathematicians

Plato believed that geometry was a discipline of pure reason and, as such, created a portal into the mind of God, who, he declared, was in the shape of an isosceles triangle. Plato was a sharp, industrious guy and was well thought of in religious circles, although on his death bed he recanted, confessing he really believed God's shape to be rhombohedron and the portal a mere orifice.

Dinostratus squared the circle, and his brother Menaechmus,

a pupil of <u>Plato</u>, doubled the cube creating new terms to go with them like *"Nina Ross on a swayback hoss,"* and *"Boxcars,"* not to mention *"Eightur from Decatur,"* and *"The Hard Way."*

<u>Archytas</u>, a friend of Plato, also was the first to double the cube, but it was a different cube. He invented the screw, but it had little practical application as his were all ten feet tall and the screwdriver was as yet unknown. Undaunted, he invented the pulley but never perfected its use in the dairy industry. His first practical invention was the rattle which he played with incessantly and sucked on to his heart's content while developing the mathematics of music, in which he proved that both Zeus and Apollo played lyres that were out of tune.

<u>Eudoxus</u> never got the fame he deserved, neither while living nor dead. He was a loner and only spoke to others when it was absolutely necessary. In his infamous autobiography, which he wrote anonymously, he continually misspelled his own name. He evidently was a very private man for when asked to recall anything he'd said, all his friends could actually remember was, *"Where's the toilet?"*

He invented proportions and made it possible to calculate the area of the sphere, but of which type we're still uncertain. Without his great mathematical insights the construction of the atomic bomb and the moon landing would have been impossible, but he's been given little credit for this by the Soviets.

Now we must hurriedly take our leave from the great scientist-mathematicians, before it gets canceled, and continue our march through the labyrinth of philosophers of the 4th century B.C.

Famous Philosophers of the 4th Century B.C.

<u>Aristippus</u> was an elegant, handsome man, wry, smooth and slick. Originally from Cyrene on the North African Coast, he studied in the Socratic School in Athens, where he was nicknamed *"Liver Lips"* by his fellow students. He loved riches, which didn't place him too far out of the mainstream of philosophic thought, and he might have been the father of what later became known as epicurianism, although, as was his custom, he would have no doubt denied his parenthood. Still, he firmly believed that he *"could possess the finer things of life*

100

without being possessed by them." What a guy! *"Everything we do,"* he said, *"is through hope of pleasure or fear of pain. Pleasure is the ultimate good and the keenest pleasures physical and sensual. The art of life is in plucking pleasures as they pass and making the most of them. The use of philosophy is to guide us to the most pleasant choice . . . and this can be accomplished by being neither the master nor slave of any man."*

Considered an abolitionist in Athens, where at least 80 percent of its occupants were slaves, he decided to leave town and travel for his health's sake. As a philosopher he was always trying to weasel money from the rich and powerful, and one day a king he was buttering up, spat on him. When his friend, who watched, asked why he put up with this, he said, *"A fisherman must put up with more moisture than this to catch a smaller mullet."* The same king asked Aristippus why philosophers seek the company of the rich, but it's never vice versa? To which he replied, *"Because philosophers know what they want, but the rich are all stupid bean-heads and vice-vermin."* When the wealthy Phrygian Simus finished escorting him proudly around his recently built ornate mansion paved with marble, Aristippus spat in his face. When his host protested, Aristippus claimed he couldn't, amidst all this beauty, *"find a more suitable place to spit."* This handsome, refined philosopher died in 356 B.C. having advanced the invention of the spittoon by two centuries.

At the same time, back in Athens, there lived a man that was a legend in his own mind, the most famous Greek philosopher of the ancient world, Diogenes the cynic. He believed, like his teacher Antisthenes, *"I do not possess in order to not be possessed"*, and considered possession nine-tenths of the law. He thought of himself as a citizen of the world but claimed it was a flat square only 250 miles across. He set up housekeeping in a tub in the courtyard of an Athenian Temple and walked about naked most of the time, engrossed in indecent acts of nature and love, and telling dirty jokes. He believed eating meat and making love were similar animal functions best done in public and eaten raw. He'd walk about at night carrying a candle, saying he was looking for an honest man, but nobody laughed, so he quit. Sometimes he dressed up like a bum and with painted face ran around giving people the finger and trying to defecate on them, but had little success, as many doubted his sincerity.

Once when captured by pirates, he was sold into slavery, but this was a big step up. His new master gave him some clothes and asked him what work he could do. *"Govern men!"* was his cryptic reply. <u>Diogenes</u> was a very popular individual and was elected to high office on many occasions but never served because of his proclivity toward sexual abuse which he believed must be practiced during all solemn occasions.

One day <u>Alexander's</u> army was marching through Corinth, armor glistening, resplendent in the sun with Alexander near its rear astride his giant <u>Bucephalus</u>. Suddenly the army came to a halt, and <u>Alexander</u> galloped to the head of the column to discover the problem. There was old <u>Diogenes</u> spread-eagled out on the road, lying in the sun naked and sweating like a chicken on election day. <u>Alexander</u> yelled at him, *"I am Alexander the Great King! Who are you?"*

"I am <u>Diogenes</u> the dog," was the enigmatic reply he gave, not moving a finger.

"Ask of me any favor you'd like." Said <u>Alexander</u> and waited in awe for a reply.

"Stand out of the sun!" <u>Diogenes</u> commanded.

The entire troop fell out and re-formed past him, and <u>Alexander</u> was heard to say, as he rode out of sight, *"If I were not the Invincible, I'd be <u>Diogenes</u>."*

It has been reported that <u>Diogenes</u> never lost an argument, although he'd sometimes act crazy in a close debate and try to urinate on his protagonist. He made much of coarse humor and wit, and once on finding an old woman kneeling with her head to the ground in front of a holy image, said, *"Are you not afraid to be in so indecent a posture, for the Gods are everywhere?"* The woman, obviously shocked, looked up and replied stoically, *"Bugger off, shit bird."* <u>Diogenes</u> lived into his nineties, evidently dying of under-indulgence.

The Skeptics

In the latter part of the 4th century B.C. philosophy took a turn toward skepticism. <u>Arcesilaus,</u> one of the finest minds, he thought, of the age said, *"Nothing is certain . . . , not even that."* But when questioned closely, he wasn't sure. Pyrrho felt that everyone had a right to his own opinion, that most everything was subjective. He said things like, *"The same object may seem small or large, ugly or beautiful and all desire is delusion,"* but still couldn't get her into the sack. When asked if he preferred life to death, he replied, *"Life is an uncertain good, death not a certain evil,"* but he never lost his doctor's phone number.

Near the end of the 4th century B.C., Epicurus moved to Rome at the age of 35. He had fallen in love with philosophy at twelve but never offered marriage. Many students of Epicurus have claimed he was an atheist, but these accusations are in doubt. They cite his statements that the aim of philosophy is *". . . to free men from fear . . . more than anything else, from the fear of Gods."* Religion, he said, *"thrives on ignorance, promotes it and darkens life with the terror of celestial spies, relentless furies and endless punishments."* Except for these few obscure quotations their arguments don't hold water, and I must admit are rather equivocal, shallow and a bit boring. After all, atheism is the most Godlike belief of all for it is undeniably obvious that logically God is an atheist, for whom can he believe in.

Epicurus went on to demolish metaphysics. *"If knowledge does not come (solely) from the senses, where else can it come from? If the senses are not the ultimate arbiters of fact, how can we find such a criterion in reason, whose data must come from the senses?"*

"It is not possible," he said, *"to live pleasantly without living prudently, honorably, and justly; nor to live prudently, honorably and justly without living pleasantly."* But he thought a stewed pig and a bucket of beer was a prudent breakfast, one obol the just payment for prostitution services, and having one's toga cleaned and pressed each week the mark of an honorable man. He did not anticipate the modern desire for *"S&M and bondage"* in his belief that pleasure is good and pain is bad, and naively thought that understanding availed in us the faculty to avoid pain. One of history's vilest acts of mendacity has been to depict Epicurus as a hedonist simply because he weighed 350 pounds. He married a whore who wrote poems. Finding them

tedious and difficult to plagiarize, he became quite jealous and said in a jejune way, *"Her purity of style does not interfere with her morals."* Yet he always considered her exceptional because she could eat a whole watermelon without spitting.

Carneades of Cyrene strutted upon the stage, a true skeptic par excellence. He would break into any person's exposition of anything whatever and demand that he *"Cut the crowing and get right to the conclusion,"* as he was quite impatient and hated details. When one obliged, he would demur, repeating his famous line, *"All conclusions are intellectually indefensible."* Once threatened by an anguished barbarian, vowing to beat his skull into liquid gism, he admitted the savage's conclusion, though still intellectually indefensible, was physically, extremely persuasive. He also married a whore, this one from Egypt, who wrote poems, and it was said of her that the purity of her style did not interfere with her morals. However, I don't believe that Carneades would agree with this estimate of his whore. He was never jealous of her and plagiarized many of her poems. Besides, she would spit on many occasions when eating; even if the only fare consisted of small figs, which, Carneades said, he fed her often.

With the end of Carneades, the *"Golden Age"* of Greek philosophers came to a close, and not a moment too soon. Other less significant Greeks followed but they had names like George Papadakis, Aristotle Onasis, and Gary Philadelphia and went into the food, shipping or cheese business at an early age.

THE SEVENTH FLAG

It was in the summer of 1841 that two men, Pancho Corrizo and Don Diego Guackgomole, embarked on an adventure that for sheer bluster, bravado, braggadocio and stupidity has no parallel, except in Texas history. Of course, today, we all know that Texas has flourished under six flags, but so has my Aunt Sadie and still no dates. Few, however, know (or care) that the people of Laredo created the *seventh* flag over Texas. They were not sure which side of the border they lived on, but neither did my uncle Babe, which partially explains why he spent his time being as revolting as possible. He wasted most of his waking hours standing in front of the movie theater on Apocalypse Ave. posing as Dubois' *"Jeanne d'Arc"* until he was arrested for female impersonation without a permit. He got off when no one could prove Jean was a girl, but then he got off often. After that, he posed as the statue of the "Manniquin Pis" and the police were stymied, then he was elected mayor. But although I tarry, I shan't dillydally, and I refuse to dwadle, mostly.

Pancho Corrizo was the bastard son of a famous Spanish noble bastard descended from a somewhat devious line of bastards going back to the famous courtesan *"Suchertorte,"* the bald mistress of King Philip III. Pancho's prized possession was a forged land grant from the King of Spain, giving him title to all the lands between the Rio Bravo and the Rio Grande. It was only much later found to be the same river; still, he was a Spanish royalist who hated and distrusted the Mexican Republic, so he plotted with his trusted confidant Don Diego Guackgomole, to rebel against Mexico's already defeated leader Santa Anna and form a new nation that he could own and rule with aplomb, and lots of it.

Don Diego was an imposing man of stature, towering over his contemporaries both in his weight and immense height. He was 5 feet tall, and weighed over 10 stones, when he could find them. The Don's burning ambition was to be a commanding general and lead brave men into combat. He felt he was ready to assume command at the drop of a hat, which he did frequently, to stay in practice. After all, he had read the *"Battles of Genghis Kahn,"* though he still thought Gengis was a Syrian. Diego had a large collection of lead soldiers that he believed were tin. He sucked on them constantly to instill fealty, but he got filthy.

On the infamous *"Noche de la Luna Roja"*, following a declaration of independence by the native peons of Laredo and surrounding vicinity, a vote was taken to create *"La Republica del Rio Grande"*, with Pancho the provisional president and Don Diego as General-in-Chief. They adjourned and advanced on the Mexican munitions depot, army stockade and tostada factory located in a small stone blockhouse in the next block. The entire garrison of six were asleep until they were awakened by the screams and shots of the thousand or so revolutionaries advancing on their base. Luckily, they were commanded by the heroic but sleeping Cápitan La Cabeza del Guano.

He awoke, screaming, *"¿Donde están los assuelos? ¿Oh, quando pueden están? ¡Hasta las armas! ¡Hasta las armas! ¡Montán a caballos y asaltos los assuelos!"* His men responded. They charged into the breach, just as the revolutionaries beat down the stockade doors, and they routed the undisciplined horde. Don Diego tried to rally his troops but unfortunately could not think of a good rally cry.

Two days later, Don Diego was riding north to Victoria to seek assistance from Mirabeau Lamar, who was supposed to be presiding at the 3rd Annual Chili Cook-off and Armadillo Festival. The Don found Lamar in an upstairs room of a rundown bordello and sausage factory reminicient of his Georgia home. Lamar was in a highly aroused state with two Indian girls and an armadillo and was incensed at the intrusion. After refusing aid to the Don, a melee ensued. Shots were fired, and the Don was forced out through the sausage machine. To make matters worse an innocent armadillo on the street was shot dead in his tracks.

After the funeral, the Don was in despair. He began eating tamales on the steps of the Helmut Dantine restaurant and manure bin. Tears welled in his eyes as his mission seemed a failure and they were out of jalapeños. At this moment, Colonel Siegfried Von Swartzercox trotted by the Don on his white stallion. This was quite a sight in Victoria, as the Don had never seen a German colonel trotting on top of a horse before. He waved and shouted his best *"Vaya Con Dios"*, which spooked the horse; it slipped and the colonel fell helmet first into the muddy street. After this, they became fast friends. Von Swartzercox was looking for revolutionary action and found in General Don Diego a revolting leader he could follow; he was always fond of following the leader, and kept calling the Don *"Mein Fuhrer."* This was a man truly ahead of his time and always thought it was at least two hours later than it was. Together they developed an amazing esprít de corps, lacking only the corps.

The next day Don Diego and the colonel began several hours of marching drill near the famous Victoria mesquite juice factory. A crowd gathered to watch on their armadillo break (instead of coffee breaks, in those early days before South America invented *"coffee to go,"* the average Texas factory worker preferred to simply walk outside and break an armadillo). The incantation of the cadence seemed to awake an elemental, primordial response in the crowd; many began to fall in behind the pathetic figures and sing martial hymns. Some, however, just fell in with bad company and were not seen 'till the next Sunday. Others began to sing marital hyms and ended up married.

The martial group marched back to Laredo, where, within a month, the Colonel had whipped them into shape and shaped them into a whip, which he would use, he declared, to *"whip"* the Mexican army. Finally, on the night of the festival of the town's patron saint, Santa Theresa of Boys' Town, Pancho Corrizo gave Don Diego his marching papers and the now hardened striking force headed south on their invasion of the Mexican heartland.

En route to Mexico City, the invaders were decimated by Gila monsters, bluebonnet plague, shoe shine boys, and the Dewey decimal system, but undaunted (except for the few, who curiously, got daunted), the army of La Republica Del Rio Grande continued inexorably toward the Capitol of Mexico. They moved rapidly for cavalry, but rarely in the right direction, and ere four years had flown, were poised on the outskirts of the enemy's stronghold.

Indians along the way had sent enchiladas ahead, warning Santa Anna of the invasion. To receive an enchilada from afar meant danger was at hand, especially if sampled. The historic confrontation took place on the ancient causeway, where the Conquistadors spilled their blood and a number of barrels of two-month-old wine. Quoting Castrate Manaléte, the chronicler of this period, *"The Causeway was strewn with human body parts, still quivering organs, and a few saxophones. The stench was sickening to all except the natives, who seemed to enjoy it immensely."*

Thousands of Mexican soldados were arranged on the Causeway. They greatly outnumbered the invaders (as they always do). Don Diego conferred with Siegfried and said, *"We are outnumbered 500 to one, but I never was good in math. I am a military man and suggest you try a frontal assault. Fight to the last man and if you have trouble, check with me for additional orders."* Don Diego then retired to his tent to weep.

Siegfried did not hesitate; he mustered his fifty best men (actually, all he had was one half-used jar of Grey Poupon). He stridently urged them to unleash their fury on the foe, but they had already latched their leeches to their leashes and left their furies in a foyer at the Stage Door Cantina. The frustrated group felt furfuration and began to delaminate until the Colonel reminded them, *"It's better to fight and win the battle than to die all cold and without clothes and all."* His impeccable logic motivated the troops to a high pitch of excitement and they rushed the bridge shouting, *"Remember Laredo and what for!"* They fought like frenzied demons and yet, within an hour, they had lost half their troops, and struggled back to reform their attack. This inspired Don Diego to send an enchilada message back to Laredo.

"Against terrible odds, our brave troops fought like frenzied demons, but it is perhaps too early to declare victory. Hold the celebration 'till you receive my next enchilada." He hurriedly dispatched the message by Indian turncoats who, after turning in their coats, used flour tortillas for their enchilada communiqués.

It was siesta time in the early afternoon when Von Swartzercox devised a diabolical plan to take advantage of his remaining army's peculiar uniforms made out of armadillo skin armor, which they wore on their backs (it made them completely invulnerable to surprise armadillo attack). The Mexicans were resting, joggling their frogs and flogging their dogs (a common army practice designed to maintain discipline). The small revolutionary army lined up in two rows of 12 and 1/2 men each. They faced backward and slowly marched toward the amazed Mexican Army. The German believed this would fool the Mexicans into thinking his attackers were in retreat, which would restore the element of surprise to his troops. The effect on the Mexicans, however, was the reverse. They thought a new type of armadillo army was attacking, although the armadillo on one soldier's back walked off, as he was still alive, though sick.

The Mexican general, Bustamante con Huevos, seeing this surprising turn of events, made the rapid decision to have his troops face the enemy and walk backwards, trying to delude them into thinking they were retreating, which they in fact were. Soon, the two armies were within the city, where they both simultaneously surrendered to each other and declared victory.

This is why history is vague and ambiguous about the seventh flag over Texas. Even today, few people are aware of the Republica Del Rio Grande <u>or</u> of Mexico.

ROCKETRY
(PROLOGUE)

One of the most bizarre and absurd coincidences in history occurred when the Johnson Space Center was sited near Clear Lake, Texas, just a *"stone's throw"* (paraclete) south of Houston. This action focused the leading edge of rocket science near the exact spot where the aboriginal natives of North America first invented Rocketry. In the year 473 B.C.C. (before cloth clothes), when leather was scarce and used only for tying crab shells together for wearing. *"Spotted Crab,"* a small, somewhat lethargic member of the Karankawa tribe stumbled across an exposed *"Aiu"* gravel bed, near Clear Lake, which was once part of the Trinity-Brazos River terraces. He was a member of a tribe of Indians who lived on Galveston Island near the Strand. It had been a particularly cold winter, and while out hunting manatees and things like that, he came near a starving black bear that chased him across the thick ice capping the bay. Now Spotted Crab didn't stop running until he stumbled across the aforementioned gravel bed. He thought of it as an *"Aiu"* bed because the pebbles were shaped like the feet of a mythical animal, common to Indian lore. The Aiu was a bird that mimicked a duck. It had the face of an owl which looked strikingly like Cole Porter, and was considered the harbinger of halcyon days if captured dead or alive, but since none had ever actually been seen, was credited with the poor state of Karankawa affairs, which never lasted over two weeks. The Aiu had feet which looked like smooth flat pebbles, and were said to smoke, drink, quack dirty words and smell like a year old bear-board.

Spot untied his crab shell loin strap, which had caused more than usual chafing from his long run. He sat on the pebble bed trying to lather things up, and then absently tied the leather strings used to secure his shells in place, into the semblance of a sling; an unfamiliar item to him, having never been to Singapore before. Unconsciously he slipped a pebble into his sling and launched it upsides a large live oak tree. Upon arriving back home, he, using the Karankawa dialect, which lacked consonants, explained and displayed his new device.

"EA, IE, I, OA, U, AAAIOU, YAAA, A-A-A, IOU, OOOOOU," he said smiling and flailing the air with his sling. The *"OOOOOU"* translates literally into *"Rock-at-Tree."* Thus, the first use of Rocketry originated near the exact spot of the present Johnson Space Center.

Even today, during rocket launches, you may hear the present natives of this land using the Karankawa *"Ooooou!"* to describe their feelings at the liftoff of a massive shuttle, harkening back down through the millennia to Spotted Crab, the man that started it all. With the mystical ties of Houston to Rocketry fresh in mind, I dedicate the following historical vignette.

A ROCKET VIGNETTE

The dark, devious and devout minds of Medieval Russian royalty committed their country to its manifold destiny, and even before the manifold was invented. The Czar suspected that Napoleon and his mincing hordes of wine stewards, chefs, waiters and taxi drivers were about to descend on Mother Russia with all their esprit de corps, panache, élan and pate de foi gras. He felt the French were intent on destroying his verdant land of borsch, potatoes and pumpernickel. Natives would be forced to eat canard a l'orange, wear funny hats, and talk with silly accents. This was all too much for the Czar of all the Russians to calmly contemplate, so when the subject came up at meetings, the Czar would frantically hop around a lot, jump, clap his hands and yell *"Woo! Woo!"* A plan was designed. (Actually it was drawn up on the house minister's drawers in the drawing room). It was drawn and quartered, and placed in the top drawer of a majestic chest of drawers. The plan appeared to draw the line against the French invaders. In essence it would place the cream of Russian scientific expertise at the disposal of Count Eelyhead Suckafinch Speransky, (the clearest head in Russia), and he would find a secret weapon to blow the French Army to smithereens (or at least numb satisfaction). Possibly a rocket or something big time like that.

Rockets weren't a new innovation in warfare. Early in 1232 when the Mongols laid siege to Kai Feng Fu, the Chinese defenders used weapons described as arrows of flying fire. Rockets were used against the Poles by the infuriated Tartar whores, or was that hordes? It's no wonder they were mad, overburdened as they were with fresh fish but with no lemons at all, as this was prior to the invention of both firearms and tartar sauce. Still, the most renowned personage in rocket history remains the famous Wan-Hu, a Chinaman. He constructed a special platform lofted by two large kites to which he attached 47 rockets that could be (and were) fired simultaneously when he was on board. His action initiated the well known "Chinaman's Chance" expression when Wan-Hu and his contrivance simply disappeared in the horrendous explosion that followed.

Rockets had three problems competing with firearms; the size of their explosive, their accuracy or stability, and the difficulty in maintaining the correct mix for the slower burning gunpowder necessary for propulsion. Because of these problems rocket development languished for centuries.

Then in 1792 Haider Ali, prince of Mysore, developed rockets flight-stabilized by a ten-foot bamboo stick (very clever those Japs). Their range was one and a half miles and were used with devastating effect on the British forces in India. The British swiftly began their own rocket manufacture and used them extensively in the early 1800's against the U.S.A., Bologne, Copenhagen and the two big *"Zig"* cities *"Leip"* and *"Dan."* The British rockets were up to 60 pounds, stabilized by 16-foot bamboo sticks, and here modern technology began to hit its limit, for rarely could rigid bamboo over 16 feet long be found. Still England was a worldwide trading country and could maintain a supply of bamboo, but what were backward countries like Russia to do where bamboo was scarce? Another way must be found! But who? What? Why? How? When? and Shit? These questions dismayed the average man on the street because their understanding of rocketry was based on Aristotelian theories of motion unsupported by fact, and it was not until near the end of the 17th century that Sir Isaac Newton published his third law of motion. Prior to this time, all research and development followed the works of the Pole Kazimierz Siemienowicz. Using his *"Artis Magnae Artilleriae, Pars Prima"* as a guide, Colonel C. Friedrich von Geissler of Germany built the world's largest rocket, made of wood, sailcloth and furniture glue. The German had problems with the glue in humid weather and the propulsion mixture burned too rapidly because of his too pure saltpeter. This account is suspect, however, as historically many men have complained of this malady.

Rocketry reached the Baltic due to the sheer chance meeting of Count Speransky and the notorious German mechanic named Grenschmeldt, when they met in a bingo parlor near Vilna. Speransky, in his memoirs written after the war, described the German as "a useful and lucky man who would fill any mechanical post admirably" and this in spite of the fact that the invention of the mechanical post still awaited the discovery of the mechanical horse. Nevertheless, he appointed Grenschmeldt his aide-de-camp. Grenschemldt held previous employment as a part time sausage stuffer and side show freak at the Bremen-Luden Shtinckelhaus und Oktoberfest foundry. He was later employed as a night watchman in Amsterdam by Captain de Boer, the famous Dutch rocket designer and inventor, who was currently experimenting with three metal vanes to eliminate the bamboo stick (or shticks as he called them).

Late one dark and stormy night, Grenschmeldt was nosing around the office searching the files under "R" for some year old Roquefort, when he espied drawings of de Boer's proposed rocket together with some filthy pictures of the local dancing

Rockettes. He was in process of copying the rocket plans while ogling the Rockettes when the cleaning woman caught him in the act. Thus compromised "Flagrante Delicto, prima facie," he was forced to both prematurely hop a boat for the Baltic and ejaculate in his pants.

He was a slow and very poor conversationalist. A horse stepped on his face when he was three, and his nose kept falling into his open mouth when he talked. It wasn't that this restricted his pronunciation; it just smelled so bad in there he had to keep stoping for air. This misfortune strengthened his character and he developed into the strong, silent type, lacking only the strength of his convictions and the ability to know when to stop babbling incoherently.

Count Speransky, the elder, who was called Count because he could, was the illegitimate son of the infamous Bastard of Muscovy, the dreaded, red headed leader of the Royal Cossack battalion and the most popular man in town until his unfortunate dismemberment at a political rally. His son, the younger Count, developed a fondness for science, and had risen to Professor of Mathematics, Physics, and Phrenology in a Moscow Seminary-Cemetery combination. His bump work drew the attention of Czarovich Alexander, and in 1802 he was assigned to the Ministry of Interior. There, he showed such capacity for hard work and intellectual repartee in interior matters (and even outside sometimes) that the Czar assigned him to direct the *"Grand Codification of Russian Limpets."* When Alexander set out for his second meeting with Napoleon in 1808, he took the younger Speransky with him as *"The only clear head in Russia."* One assumes he meant other than the Czar himself, but perhaps not, in retrospect, taking into account the events that unfolded.

War with Napoleon threatened early in 1811, and the Czar appointed Speransky to head a new department in charge of secret weapons and their development. This at first confused "the only clear head" which, even Speransky himself, would have admitted was clear mainly because it was almost empty...not of facts, figures, nor of real substance, but empty of nuances, ambiguity, and paradox, empty of fine shades of meaning. This resulted in a miserably understated semantic mix up, not uncommon in this period, since "semantics" had not yet been spelled correctly.

His first approach to this assignment may appear peculiar to us now, looking back over the centuries from our present lofty vantage point, built up over years of painstaking scientific research and history, but at the time it was considered a farsighted and bold experiment. He supervised the construction of a small laboratory in which was built an impressive array of secret hiding places. In these, he placed various ordinary weapons: handguns, rifles, swords, chicken hooks, etc. and waited expectantly. Unfortunately, when the second quarter budget was applied for, it was discovered that this approach to developing secret weapons; i.e., hiding various weapons in secret places to see what would develop, was not at all what the Czar had in mind. Speransky was summarily dispatched to search the countryside for new weapons. He first traveled toward the Baltic and one night found himself in argument with the bingo player across the table over the small pile of bits of purple cabbage leaves they were using to mark their cards. It was Grenschmeldt, who mistakenly thought the cabbage was his personal supply of crudities, or Russian Cole slaw. During the heated argument which ensued, Grenschmeldt inquired as to the Russian's desire to have a small rocket stuffed up one of his particularly vulnerable orifices and get launched to Lake Ladoga. Suddenly, Speransky realized this man might have some knowledge of rockets, a decidedly secret weapon, since he'd never heard of them before, and by the end of the night a proposition had been offered by Speransky and accepted by Grenschmeldt, although the German exhibited a certain reticence, having never accepted a proposition from a man before.

Within a month, Grenschmeldt and a platoon of Russian engineers, hand picked by Speransky off the most complicated road construction jobs in Russia, were installed in the Goniff Gun-powder and Cosmetic Combine located ten miles upstream from one of Russia's major cities. Coincidentally, on June 27, 1812, Napoleon began the long trek from Kovno to Moscow.

Grenschmeldt encountered a series of start up personnel and organizational problems in the first two weeks of his rocket construction operation. He had an aversion to Russian food and language, and did not like the native tongue. He preferred to eat bratwurst, sauerbraten, and liechtenstein instead. He couldn't speak one word of the language, and resented the fact that the natives spoke only Russian, their native tongue, which as previously mentioned he despised; though he liked tonguing the natives, and life was at least bearable, in spite of the fact that when questioned in Russian he would invariably reply. "No schplich, no schplich Rooskie."

Strangely, as time passed, the Russians began to refer to all Germans as "Schplichs." Undeterred, he would constantly exhort his workers and soldiers to heightened activity, grabbing his nose and yelling, "Shmantzes! Der rakkuktschmekles und der eibenlickker vill splachalatzen uff der froggengrubber schwienders."

Within two months the threat to Moscow had become acute, and the Russian army of the north rallied around Speransky's rocket works. Grenschmeldt's men had completed construction of 675,328 rockets: all 100 pounders with three curved metal vane stabilizers and six sets of thirty copper tube launchers. Napoleon's Grand Armee broke the Russian lines at Borodino, and panic swept over the Czar's commanders. They called on Speransky before his field testing was complete, and under direct orders from the Czar, had the rockets loaded on troikas for rapid transport to the southeast in a belated attempt to flank the French. At the appointed place on the edge of the tree line, well hidden along the invasion route, Grenschmeldt supervised the setting up of the launchers in wait to ambush the French. Speransky was so confident of success that he had sent invitations to the Czar and General Kutzov to witness the first use of his secret weapons. They all met, told a few jokes and settled down to have lunch and wait for the enemy.

The Czar had grown to rely heavily on Kutzov. He considered him his best general and had him accompany him wherever he went. Alexander became very suspicious of everyone in 1812 after the war started and felt he was being followed everywhere. For the last six months he rode backwards on his horse. He believed an assassination attempt was imminent and even had his dog Sasha searched three times a day for firearms. The Czar trusted Kutzov alone; Kutzov would taste the Czar's wine and food before he would eat or drink; before making love to the Empress, Kutzov had to first. The Czar became truly paranoid after the defeat at Boradino and would not take off his clothes at night until Kutzov stripped. In the mornings Kutzov had to scratch, yawn and relieve himself before the Czar would, but I deviate, though it's none of your business (unless you're one).

Thirty rockets were hand selected by Grenschmeldt for the first volley, and on that Indian summer's day Speransky, astride his white mare, took personal command of the launchers. Slowly, over a grassy knoll, helmets glistening brightly in the sun, their smashing red, white and blue uniforms forming an awe inspiring sight, the French army marched into view, and Speransky, with faint trepidation, waited until the entire host was within range and spread out before them in perfect flanking position for a suprise attack. He then, winking at the Czar, gave the order to fire that fateful first salvo, and Grenschmeldt began running back and forth down the line of rockets with a large red glowing log of punk at the ready, maniacally screaming, "Splachalatzen der Froggen-grubber schwienders!"The missiles were fired!

"The rockets proceeded beautifully in majestic grandeur for 100 steps." Speransky later related, "and they left beautiful trails of smoke and fire which caused great panic in the ranks of the previously proud French Army." His eyewitness account ends here as the rockets started zig-zagging crazily, turning back on the Russians and their steeds with unbearably chaotic results. Panic spread now; not only among the French, but the Russians also. The Czar's grey stallion "Pupu" bolted and he fell into a large tub of gefilte fish brought specially for the occasion. General Kutzov lost his control, and wet his pants, much to the consternation of his steed. Speransky had been hit on the head by one of the rockets and was out cold, which he considered a desirable state and spent his remaining years in Siberia where he would be out cold most of the time.

Napoleon, while watching these surprising events unfold,

began to laugh with derision, but his laughter turned to consternation when he saw Grenschmeldt, foaming at the mouth while running and lighting rockets, screaming:

"Gotterdammerung Froggen Schwine!"

He stopped at the last rocket in his battery, lit it and then ran with it in his arms until it and he headed skyward. His added weight seemed to stabilize the missile and it gracefully headed on a perfect arc, with Napoleon on the earthward end of its chord. Suddenly, at the rocket's apogee, the propellant was spent, and the rocket and Grenschmeldt seemed suspended in an eerie limbo, appearing as some kind of religious vision, a mystical apparition of the first order. The panic stricken troops momentarily stopped to genuflect, except for the Jews who flicked their ginnys and fiddled on the roof. Swiftly the magic moment was gone, and Grenschmeldt, astride the missile, headed earthward straight toward Napoleon who was now running in circles shouting "Sacre Blue! Mon Dieu! Le Grand Merde! La Sangre Cour du Lac! Besa me cula!" Everyone waited with bated breath (but no live bait was used).

To Napoleon's relief, Grenschmeldt and the rocket landed harmlessly several feet away. Harmless that is, to everyone except the German and the rocket. It was impossible to tell where the rocket ended and the Kraut's body began; they were melded together into what appeared to be some modern Chicago sculpture of springtime. At one time hundreds of rockets were flying erratically in all directions, and Napoleon later decided, while the Russian army could not thwart his invasion, (actually only one person was killed in the entire episode, Grenschmeldt) Russia was a land of unstable, unreliable and slightly uncivil disobedient individuals impossible to govern by military occupation.

Back at the rocket base, the several hundred thousand remaining rockets, flawed by the erratic curves of their stabilizers, were never again used. They were precipitously dumped into the river by the peace loving peasants who lived nearby. Ultimately the saltpeter from these rockets, now estimated at over 36,000 metric tons drifted downstream and polluted the city's drinking water supply for thirty-three years.

The city's name was changed by this calamity, and for a century and a half was called by its now historical name, "Salt Petersburg."

THE LOOMING GLOWER IN THE

GLOAMING

It's a hot night in Houston that July in 1960, and I am sorting through my mail when I spy a letter, the postmark of which is (gulp) Belgium. I pluck it out of the stack and lo and behold it's from Ice Cream. He is in Antwerp at the annual Twerp Festival, and as he is one of the more far out characters I know, I open the letter on the spot. And the spot, by the way, is a very good one, as it is in the well-lit but still dingy library at the back end of my adobe abode.

Now Ice Cream is a rather different character, and one who thinks deep thoughts about things most people won't spend two seconds on, but I find many of them quite amusing, as he has a way with words and phrases that I admire and distrust. I find I like them even more when I can understand what they're all about, but with his erratic mind-set; this is not always possible. Still, sometimes you just have to go with the sounds and flow of his words. The letter starts this way.

"If I didn't know that I didn't know. I'd think that I knew; and if I didn't know that I knew, I'd think that I didn't know."

Well I'm hip to his rather bizarre penchant for paradoxical phrases so I give this short shrift and plug along.

"Now let's say that there is something that I'm supposed to know (in other words I don't know what it is I don't know, and yet am supposed to know). This makes me feel that I look stupid, seeming both not to know it and not knowing what it is I don't know. Therefore I pretend that I know it! This can be nerve racking, since I don't know what I must pretend to know. But there is a solution! I pretend to know everything!"

But of course, he's always doing that. As far back as I can remember he pretends to know everything except for math, science, mechanics and auto differentials. Nevertheless, he now makes this statement, so I decide to go on and see where he leads.

"Now when I encounter a truly brilliant person, such as you, I feel that you know what I am supposed to know, but that you can't tell me what it is, because you don't know that I don't know what it is."

Wow, his attempt at gratuitous flattery strangely works wonders with me. Against my better judgment, I somehow inflate up quite a bit by his remark on my brilliance. Specially, since no one else ever describes me that way. I say hardly ever 'cause I do now recall my doting grandma who, when I am five, watching me pick a scab off of my knee causing the blood to flow, uses the word brilliance in her sarcastic description. Nonetheless I now feel quite capable of making sense of whatever lies ahead in this letter, so with great confidence I determine to forge onward at full speed.

"See, guy, you may know what I don't know, but not that I don't know it, and I can't tell you, 'cause if I could, I'd tell me. So, the only thing that we can do is have you tell me everything. I mean, like, Irving can see that he sees what Melvin can't see, and Irving can see that Melvin can't see that Melvin can't see it. So Irving, seeing that he sees what Melvin can't see, nevertheless must see that he can't see that Melvin doesn't see that Melvin can't see it. Irving tries to get Melvin to see that Irving can see what Melvin can't see, but still Irving can't see that Melvin doesn't see that he can't see it."

Now I'll admit to a bit of slippery reasoning through this section, but after all, it's all in pretty small words and I vow to read it again someday and clear up any minor mysteries that lie in his strange and, at times, indecipherable communications.

"Face it, Irving knows there is something Melvin doesn't know. I know you can see that; in fact, I see that you now know that I and Melving are solving the whole problem, while you and Irving are serving merely to compound the problem. But how would you two have known that? He not knowing what it was that you don't know, and you not knowing what it was that he didn't know - - not to mention the further complications which would arise if we considered the fact that we didn't know what either or both of you knew we knew or what you knew we knew about what the both of you knew.

"Knowing, not knowing, substituting pretension, requiring one and all to move slowly but inexorably from the simple truth to complex perfidy. This is the crux of the issue. This is not a silly story of one or two or two groups, only the sad, pitiful chronicle of man's turbulent history on our abused planet's surface. For example: The USA is afraid of Russia; Russia is afraid of the USA. The U.S. is more afraid of Russia if the USA thinks that Russia thinks that the USA is afraid of Russia. Russia in turn is more afraid of the USA if Russia thinks that the USA thinks that Russia is afraid of the USA. Since the USA is afraid that Russia will think that the USA is afraid, the USA pretends that they are not afraid of Russia, so that Russia will be more afraid of the USA, and since Russia is afraid that the USA will think that Russia is afraid, Russia pretends that they are not afraid of the USA. Is it possible that eventually both will become frightened of being frightened and of frightening each other, instead of being frightened not to be frightened and not to frighten? Can the USA and Russia, terrified that each other are not terrified become terrified that each is terrified and eventually not terrified that they not be terrified?

"I don't know, but I now realize that this is the thing I wanted to know whether I knew. I felt that you probably knew what it was that I didn't know and could perhaps know what to tell me. If not, then just pretend you know everything and tell me everything. If not don't tell me anything and I'll tell you everything. Love, Ice."

Reading certain parts of his letter is like hauling big buckets of manure up a hill. About the only good thing you can say about them all when the job is done is that they are all fresh. Silly as it is, I must admit that Ice correctly depicts the *"humanity aspect"* of the cold war down to the *"T."* His insights, which he cloaks in strange silly ways, somehow bear the stamp of truth, I believe. At least sometimes I feel I believe.

A few days later another letter from Ice appears on my desk. This time I decide to wait for some quiet time in the middle of the night to open it. Feeling that I may need a certain period of undisturbed meditation to get through it in a more down to earth manner than the last one. When I open it I see that this letter is quite different. It begins this way.

"I will begin with my philosophy, which I think is only fair. I have been widely misunderstood and misquoted, and I feel a clear simple statement of my beliefs will clarify the situation considerably. I also hope that this will in some way stimulate you to write me your thoughts occasionally but be careful because I am easily over-stimulated.

1. Paradoxical premise cannot exist in an orderly universe (it hurts my feelings to admit this).
2. Fleeting glimpses of truth are often misconstrued as lapses of sanity; this has got to be since I am not only truthful but also insanitary, hopefully insane and also lapsed.
3. An asexual approach to roaches precludes all attempts at prolonging your anal ego. This kinda hurts me to reveal this, but I'm leveling.
4. Good will, though intangible, is the very firmament of man's attempt to solace his soul with gratitude; so why not go out and do everything you can about this?
5. Money cannot beget evil, since money is perversion tantamount to undisturbed tautology in itself. I used to know a lot more about this, but I've been busy and feel a bit sick too.
6. Attempts to flood your closeness of person with neglect of generosity end in nakedness of purpose. You can go too far with this avenue of thinking, but do.
7. Once in the moment of a rare dream, I pictured a fair virgin who was at one with nature, but I never made out with her again.
8. Trying to erase the richness of past painful experiences is indeed unwise and not unlike throwing chickens at Mexicans in wintertime.
9. Look around you. Look at life, nature, at the wonderful symmetry of design and balance of it all. Then can you still ask if there is a God? A Creator? No, because you wonder . . . Whom would you ask? What would you ask? When would you ask? Where would you ask?

How much would you ask? How fast? How hot? How cold would you ask? Would you ask? Would you tell? Could you? Could you KU? Cud-yu, cud-yu, cud-yu, KU? Has anybody seen my God? Turned up robe, rules the globe, really knows just when to probe. Has anybody seen old God? Five-foot thick, no mere hick, talk about the biggest dick, has anybody seen that guy?"

Now I'm just amazed how Ice can lay out his entire philosophy of life to me in a mere nine steps. Come to think about it, his is the only philosophy of life I know of all my friends and acquaintances. Matter of fact, I never even figure out what mine is, so you can see how impressive this appears to me. I spend the rest of the next two days reviewing my thoughts and feelings trying to figure out what my philosophy of life is, if any. Next, I attempt to write it out, although, I'm still not sure if I got it all figured out right. This takes me about two hours and 36 minutes and 12 seconds give or take a couple quarters and a two-bit piece, and then I reread it or try to. I find this is not only a mental gymnastic event but also a physical one, since it was just next to illegible, and therefore ineligible. I find it takes me two hours and 36 minutes and 12 seconds to read it, give or take a couple of chicken necks and a drumstick or two. Later I immediately transcend into a state of nirvana and spend the rest of the evening sort of nerving in and out of my own vernacular, sorting out the flotsam and jetsam as I nerv. I finally realized that I couldn't tell if I was really serious or just serious, and when I finished I threw it all in the wastebasket to signify defeat. However even the wastebasket wouldn't accept it and threw it back at me to signify its indomitable spirit when it comes to trash. After all there's trash and trash!

I believe there is no such word as *"can't."* Yet I believe in a guy named Kant and a thing called *"cant."* Then why can't I write it all down and make it sing? Well, evidently I can, I just don't like the lyrics, but that's okay because I believe in don't. I also believe in won't, but that's neither here nor there. Then why *"I before E except after C?"* Could that mean that it's <u>niether</u> here nor there? It's simply that the things Ice says are always *"sperm"* of the moment events. His mind seems to get completely away from sex on only rare occasions, and then it's when mine is on it. Still who can tell what actual action one might take when the situation presents itself?

I remember a night long ago when I have a blind date with a big fat girl named *"Fats."* Repellency seems to paint itself all over me by her fat when I first glimpse this moving mountain of flesh, but before the night is over I find I fall head over heels in squish with her and begin squishing her all over the place. Not squeamish I. I squeeze her squishy, squdgy, squatty, squash till it squeals like a squad of squirming squid. Things are getting better and better until suddenly she squishes me off, which feels better than it sounds, though maybe not, but then I experience much shame, guilt and a lot of squooshiness all over my body. Maybe I am too squirrely. Who knows? Definitely not me, and I'll deny it as long as I live.

Suddenly I find myself locked into a mental logorrhea, whipping round and round in an ever-increasing speeding vortex of mental abstraction (like a Nazi on speed). Even my delusions of grandeur grow exponentially. Thank heaven the exponent is the natural and not the common one. I'm making a fast pass around the perimeter of the spinning ellipsoid. I'm falling into a black hole, a labyrinth of darkness surrounding my lost sanity, when I black out from the centrifugal (or is it centripetal) forces that tug at my turgid brain. When I awake I know just what the bottom of the barrel looks like and who's down there with me. I'm sure that with the correct treatment I'll be back writing proper stories in a few months. Just one thing though, all my letters from Ice Cream will be censored by my shrink from now on.

THE LAAhNZ

The history of Houston is replete with stories of fabulous men, of corporate giants, fabulous plans and major projects of the entrepreneurial spirit. The man-made ship channel, the massive petrochemical infrastructure, the world famous Medical Center are all facets of a city considered the most dynamic of those resting on the southern coast of our fair land. Strange and wondrous tales of the city abound, of the men, ideas, and coincidental circumstances associated with many commercial enterprises, bold in conception and execution in this bayou city. Thousands of small dramas survive to this very day. They are told and retold till they become the stuff legends are made of. This is the tale of one of these. Not a weighty story of far reaching strength or precise planning; nor is it one that encompasses the passion, tenderness and terror of the human condition. The characters in it are neither brave nor bold, grand nor great, exceptional nor brilliant. They are of common clay, like your own neighbors . . . almost. But they march together in a bizarre enterprise of such problematic value that to ignore the happening would be a crime of omission teetering on the brink of calamity, and tottering in the sink of calumny.

This tale is true. Only the names, places, and times may have been changed to protect the guilty from the innocent. Innocent of what, you may ask, but than again you may not.

In Texas lore there is an area of the coastal plain between Houston and Victoria where highway #59 runs parallel to the old Houston to Victoria railroad line. The story goes that a string of towns lie on this highway. They were originally water stops for the area's first railroad. A famous old conductor or engineer of this train is said to have named these stops after his daughters. They are all small Texas towns now, and a glance at the map will display his daughter's names; Inez, Edna, Louise, and Ganado. Our story concerns a famous ranch not far from one of these towns.

It was a hot night that June in 1969, and the LAAhNZ Brothers were meeting together in the living room of a residential abode in southwest Houston. The "brothers," Bobo, Dago and Cal, each with different last names, were meeting to plan the future of their recent joint purchase, the fabled LAAhNZ Ranch.

"Hey, guys, did you see the write up in the Gladny Times-Herald on us? You could have knocked me over with a feather when I saw it."

Cal was all smiles as he waved the clipping in the air right in front of their noses. This forty-year-old scientist of medium height with dark-brown hair and eyes, a bit stocky, with a broad freckled face was obviously pleased with the activity to date.

"I don't think I'm much interested in the Gladny Times-Herald," Dago responded, "It's a newspaper isn't it? I'm not much interested in reading newspapers. They all seem rather common to me."

Dago, a tall handsome veterinarian who recently married into one of Texas' most famous wildcatter families, evidently considered newspaper reading a poor form of entertainment. He was a couple years younger than the other two men were.

"Well, I'm sorta partial to hearing it, if you don't mind, if it don't take too long." Bobo interjected. Bobo was a short, wiry intensely active MD who headed the "Number One Medical Clinic" in his hometown. Known locally as Doctor P.P., he built the clinic especially to treat "number one" problems. He spent years overseas on secret government medical projects of a highly restricted and provocative nature, many of which are unmentionable.

"Okay," Cal said, "Since you both want to hear it that much, I'll read it out loud to you. This may give you an appreciation of the mystic ties we have with the past, and will also allow me to listen to myself speaking out loud in my own inimitable way, which I might add, I enjoy immensely. Ah emmh, emmh!"

"Must you always clear your throat like that before you speak? I find the sound greatly distressing and impossible to duplicate, besides I'm a crossword puzzle buff and don't know how to spell the sound you just made," Dago replied testily.

"No interruptions, please," Cal remarked, standing. "In one of the most bizarre coincidences in modern Jackson County history, deed records regularly perused by our crack reporters, turned up the startling fact that the fabled LAAhNZ Ranch circa 1936 was recently purchased from its former owners by the LAAhNZ Brothers of Alvin and Houston.

"We had no previous knowledge of the brothers' whereabouts, and believe only time will tell what changes will be made to this famous county resort."

"Hey," said Dago, "That is sort of a coincidence, hmmm, never thought of it that way before."

"Yeah," intoned Bobo. "Now that you think about it, strange coincidences like that aren't supposed to happen. Makes you want to recheck Nostradamus or the Saturday Evening Post."

The men, all around forty, recently pooled their meager resources and their State Veteran's Land Board benefits to jointly strike a deal with Slick Cruekshank, infamous Jackson County Realtor and bon vivant. They purchased the place "sight unseen." Sure, they had heard of the mysterious LAAhNZ in Texas lore but only as a fantasy, like Camelot. They didn't know it was in Jackson County. They thought it was in Europe or Beaumont.

Two weeks before this meeting Bobo explored the place. It was mostly a flat, featureless plain covered by oak and yupon, with a bunch of senderos cut through it for deer hunting. Bobo declared that nobody would have ever heard of Ozymandias should his monument area lie as barren of ruins as the LAAhNZ. No one could find a trace of its former greatness. He then reported that the remainder of his time was spent exploring the eastern end of the ranch, which later received the name of the "black swamp." This palmetto and scrub oak lowland appeared constantly murky and damp, probably due to its proximity to two neighboring features: 1. A flat and almost perpetually flooded rice paddy to the north, and 2. A rather deep one acre tank, complete with concrete pier and 21 foot cabin cruiser, immediately to the east.

Then Bobo smiled mysteriously, and smugly said that he

found, and with no little effort, extracted a rather large decaying wooden sign that he only noticed because of the protruding remains of an African rhinostrich carving on the top of the sign. It poked up about six inches above the damp swamp.

As you are probably aware, the African rhinostrich is a popular mythological animal that rivals the unicorn and Chinese dragon in its mythological popularity. It has the body of a large rhinoceros and the head and neck of an ostrich, and when frightened has a tendency to bolt off at about 30 knots. The momentum of this ponderous mass and its accelerating velocity is awe inspiring, but if the beast truly panics it will thrust its head into the sand while still in full flight, immediately breaking its neck and expiring on the spot. This partially accounts for its rarity in the geo, zoo-o, and biological records. The beauty and wonder of its nature seems due to its staid, aloof, dispassionate and imperturbable temperament. Nothing frightens it. Guns, loud noises, mighty nearby earth eruptions, other animals, rapidly rising water, fire; nothing upsets its even nature, except the sight of another rhinostrich. I presume that this was the prime reason Hannibal traveled with elephants instead, on his Alpine crossing, heralding the first successful invasion of Rome.

By way of a postscript, I may add that the rhinostrich is flightless. But I digress. Huh?

With great labor and a sharp shooter, Bobo finally unearthed the sign and deciphered the old English lettering, which used a lot of F's where S's should have been. Then he proceeded to regale the other brothers with quotes from it.

Bobo finished his description of the sign, leaned back in his easy chair as a smile of wonderment and sweet satisfaction spread across his fair visage. He awaited a reaction from the brothers.

"There were giants in those days," said Dago.

"Wow, what a bunch of erudite gentlemen our forefathers were," Cal added.

"Yeah!" Dago chimed in; "They could really call a spade a spade."

"What's that mean?" yelled Bobo, suddenly squinting at Dago with a look of paranoiac distrust, "Why did you call me a spade; what's a spade?"

"A card," Dago replied calmly. "That's where your nickname comes from, Ace!"

"Why call a spade a spade? Sounds pretty imprudent to me, you bigot," Bobo yelled.

"Don't go crazy again, Ace, us brothers got to stick together come hell or high water," Cal interjected.

"There you go again, prognosticating and pontificating. How much can a brother stand before the shooting starts and all your warts fall off?" Bobo screamed.

"If I had two chickens I'd stuff 'em down both your throats," Dago yelled, then retrospectively, "but then I wouldn't have any to stuff up my ass."

"Okay, okay, brothers," said Bobo, mellowing, "The first thing we've got to do is restore the sign and put it up at the gate. We've got to build one at the LAAhNZ entrance."

They agreed to build the gate. There was no fence to tie it to, but Cal and Dago vowed to put in a gate anyway. The sign would come next. Admonishments from the old sign mentioned Spot, the rhino, so the brothers started formulating revalidation plans. They rented a large-covered trailer and drove through Edna with red and white "The LAAhNZ" signs on both sides, and a big "Danger: Rabid and Vicious Animal" sign on the back. This was their initial attempt to convince the local gentry that Spot was returning to the LAAhNZ.

Two weeks passed and then around noon on Saturday, Dago and Bobo were inside the trailer with a bass drum, and two large tubs of yellow dyed ammonia water and a baseball bat. In downtown Edna, when pedestrian traffic was near its peak, the car and trailer stopped in the heart of town at one of the two main intersections. On a signal from Cal, the driver, the others shook the trailer, beat on the drum, and generally made a big racket, then they dumped one tub of water at each intersection. The water ran out the back of the trailer onto the street in a deluge. After a couple of slow circles around town the car and trailer disappeared in the direction of the LAAhNZ to the curious delight of the talkative townsfolk.

One month later on a trip to inspect Lake Chimene and the

Great LAAhNZ oak, the brothers stopped for gas at a station just outside El Campo. While filling up Dago entered into the following conversation with the attendant:

"Hey, man, how far are we from the LAAhNZ?"

"The what?"

"You know, the LAAhNZ, that world-famous resort west of Edna."

"Hmmm, yep, I've heard of it but never heard about it. I've never checked the mileage. Uh! Sure sorry bout that."

In a tone dripping with disgust and disbelief, Dago said, "You mean to tell me you don't know the distance to the number one attraction in the area? I guess not too many people stop at this station, huh?"

The attendant had a stunned, quizzical, hangdog expression on his face as the brothers sped off.

About three weeks later in a different car, the brothers stopped again at the same station and asked the same question. This time the attendant said, "Hey, everybody's asking about that place. It's about 10 miles west of Edna on highway 822. It's one of the most popular places in the state. My wife and I are planning a vacation there in the near future."

Bobo and his wife Shorty camped out on the north end of the LAAhNZ later that summer, trying to clear the swamp environs of underbrush. They both threw themselves into the task without let up, but at the end of two weeks, only small accomplishments were evident. They were both tanned and rugged looking when they appeared back in civilization to relate their experiences. Although they glowed with that healthy bronzed outdoorsy look and Bobo's eyes still sparkled with determination and grit, one could not help noticing the scratches, bruises and welts all over their bodies, no doubt the result of their ordeal with the insect hordes that considered the swamp their home. One got the feeling of a transitory passing from one emotional state to another when Shorty, Bobo's wife, began to describe the end of each day. She spoke in glowing terms about how Bobo climbed up a wooden platform and dumped a bucket of cold water down on her for her nightly shower, the high point of her day. No doubt Bobo and Shorty's love of the LAAhNZ had diminished quickly to the point of no return.

Next Cal, his wife and three young sons, 10, 8, and 5 packed up a camping trailer with shotguns and supplies. Using Bobo's jeep, they headed for an Easter holiday at the LAAhNZ. They arrived at dusk and drove immediately into the Black swamp where the four-wheel-drive vehicle got stuck fast. It sank rapidly to floorboard depth in the morass.

Nature is a wonderful and glorious thing, but sometimes manifests its incompatibility with man's machines in a rather blatant manner. The slosh of muddy boots and hands on fresh linen and blankets created a rather depressing milieu in the otherwise pristine and placid environment.

They spent the next morning digging the car out, prying the wheels out of the muck, and spent the rest of the day setting up camp and cleaning up from their initial muddy encounter. The second morning found the happy little group sitting around the breakfast fire enjoying a hearty meal. The three children finished first and ran joyfully into the woods. There they began thrashing around in the underbrush to their hearts' content, while their parents savored second cups of coffee.

Cal had a trace of theater and a touch of intellectual pomposity in his personality. He was city born and bred but had spent a great deal of time in the country. He considered himself quite knowledgeable in rustic skills and exuded a complete competence and know-how of the Texas countryside. Now that I come to think about it, he acted that way about everything else. It was quite natural, when the small boys began yelling about a snake in the underbrush that his wife, Buzzin said, "Big daddy, you'd better go watch those kids and keep them away from the snake; they might get hurt."

Well, Big Daddy reluctantly left his remaining coffee on a nearby stump and leisurely strolled the thirty yards or so into the underbrush where the youngsters clustered about a large yupon bush. He was in no hurry. After all, he had three sons, two of which were expendable at any specific moment in time. They were bleating excitedly about the snake, so in fine western style, Big Daddy strode up between the boys and the bush, laying on that protective fatherly attitude children love, and placing himself between the danger and his beloved offspring. The theater of this "little piece of cake" was not lost on Big Daddy; he knew snakes. He gently told the boys to back off.

"Now boys," he said, reaching down to pick up the stick he saw lying near his foot. "Just where'd yawl see the snake?"

Before the answer came, Big Daddy knew the question to be moot as he felt the fangs clamp onto his right hand. This was immediately followed by the sensation of a burning acid-like fluid, painful enough to convince even a brain dead New Yorker that the snake bite was from one of those poisonous varieties Texas is famous for.

"Yawh! Wow! Yeehow!" The bellow reverberated through the woods, it stopped grazing deer in their tracks, if any; rabbits froze in mid bound to change the direction of their travel; even the snake appeared stunned by the resonance and remained stock still at his feet, its venom spent.

"Sheee it!" He murmured, beginning to calm down, but all the while thinking that his luck had changed. He moved back toward the campfire and calmly and in low tones said, "Keep away from that damn copperhead kids, and Buzzin have you got a knife?" Big Daddy was determined now to slice the mandatory X's over the fang marks and suck out the venom, as he had been taught to do thirty years before when he was a boy scout in mighty troop 70. He was solicitously presented with an old cheap foot-long butcher knife that got its last sharpening eight years ago in preparation for some linoleum cutting. It had a worn wooden handle and a wide flexible blade. He hastily placed his right hand on a stump and began trying to saw an "X" over the first fang mark.

"Damn," he thought, "I'd give my right arm to be left-handed." With much pain and difficulty he finally succeeded with the first "X," while the kids watched in fascination and yelled their support, although the limited alphabet attempted was somewhat disappointing to them.

By the time he found the second fang mark his élan and determination slackened appreciably; he felt the cold sweat on his face and the nauseated feeling in his stomach. The theatrics suddenly seemed unimportant now, and he said, "Buzzin, I think

I'm ready for you to run me into town and find a saw bones."

The last thing the adults did prior to leaving, was to line up the kids and make them each swear to stay away from the guns and "leave that damn snake alone" till they got back. Buzzin drove to Edna to a young doctor's office where they together learned the modern method of handling snakebites. My, how techniques have changed over the years.

First a shot to deaden the pain, then a miniature very sharp auger to cut the meat out around the fang holes, which according to the Doc, contained about 75% of the poison. This induced a bit of blood letting which was supposed to flush out most of the remaining 25%. Finally Buzzin drove to Ganado where Big Daddy checked into a hospital room for observation.

Buzzin next high-tailed it back to the kids. They, true to their natures, if not their promises, as soon as their parents were out of sight, grabbed the shotguns and blew the snake to smithereens. They later insisted that they must bring the remains to show to Big Daddy in the hospital, which they did, much to his chagrin, as he realized he was not only hospitalized but also one upped by his kids. A slackening of the LAAhNZ's unbridled appeal now claimed another brother. Two down, one to go.

Dago solved his problem in a more civilized manner. He just never stayed there long enough for the sun to set; consequently his love of the place lasted longest. It was a festive occasion when with great pride the brothers finally raised the new though slightly different sign next to the LAAhNZ gate. The black and white letters were in a modern script now, but readable from at least 50 feet and quite an impressive item. It listed under the large "Welcome to the LAAhNZ, the Xanadu of the southwest," the following rules and regulations:

1. Do not feed "Spot" the rhinoceros.
2. No wallowing aloud!
3. 15 cents riffraff exclusion fee.
4. No hunting and fishing prohibited.
5. All trash and excrement must be buried to a depth of five feet or less. This means YOU!
6. Absolutely no pets allowed on the ranch. No dogs or cats allowed. Sheep are okay, okay?

7. No exfoliating in season!
8. No Treading! All treaders will be forcibly removed if possible.
9. All trespassers will be prosecuted to the limit of the LAAhNZ.
10. Billiard drinkers not allowed in the poolroom.
11. Remember this is your LAAhNZ (sorta). Moral deportment required. Horse lovers are not allowed to sleep in the barn.

A year later the brothers initiated a new project, "Mouth Park," a pocket sized parcel of land near downtown Houston. They designed a four-story, four-sided monument of a mouth in four designs. East Mouth, West Mouth, North Mouth and of course the piece de resistance, South Mouth. They intended to donate the park to the City of Houston in partial recognition for their continuing love affair with big H.

Problems arose however, when the City Council balked over an explicit codicil of the deed, which stated, "Should the monument be defaced in any manner, the brothers or their heirs have the right, at their sole discretion, to reclaim the entire parcel."

With one last LAAhNZ Brothers' quote, I now close the book on this endeavor, the likes of which I'm sure I'll never witness again, nor most likely will you.

"Many years have now passed since the we stood on the point where the LAAhNZ sign stands to remind us all of the glories of the past. Yet these bittersweet memories will always remind us of the LAAhNZ, the LAAhNZ, and again the LAAhNZ."

NOBLESSE OBLIGE

It was a hot night in Houston that late October Sunday night in 1944, and Toad, baggage in hand, was hurrying down the tunnel connecting Houston's Grand Central Station to the various train platforms and gates where passengers boarded and departed incoming and outgoing passenger trains. This second semester freshman was headed for westbound gate number eight, the temporary resting place of the overnight local to Austin, the state Capitol and lodgment of the University of Texas. He planned to board his coach early, hoping to find a roomy spot for a comfortable night's sleep before morning classes, as the train was scheduled to arrive at 5:30 the next morning.

The sticky air in the tunnel had that sooty, acrid smell familiar to all rail travelers. Recently 17, he thought it not unpleasant; it conjured up feelings of the mechanized progress of man, the future of invention, discoveries awaiting just around the bend, and exciting visions of adventure. The slick, bright, multicolored Hawaiian style rayon shirt he wore fluttered all over in the steady breeze constantly blowing through the tunnel as he moved down the spacious dark concrete and tile incline. Khaki pants, swishing time to his steps, imperceptibly triggered the beat, then the music, and finally the words of Russ Morgan's popular "There Goes that Song Again" in his brain. He began to quietly sing it as he walked in steady cadence. The soft sounds from his lips were punctuated by syncopated heavy breathing as he ascended the ramp to the ground level tracks, but diminished to near silence as the other waiting passengers came into view near the top of the incline. He had now arrived on the broad concrete walkway separating two resting olive drab metallic monsters; their only signs of life being occasional bursts of white steam below their dark undersides and a bit of light from their dimly lit interiors.

Looking down the platform area hoping to see his coach's number, he noticed the knot of Army Air Force personnel to the right. Rumpled uniforms gave stark but mute testimony that their owners had seen a great deal of the town on weekend passes. The loud harsh laughs, cryptic innuendoes, and grating sounds of their speech had an irritating effect on the boy as he passed.

"New Yorkers, no doubt," he thought, as his eyes darted past to gaze on the more familiar sights of lightly colored cotton dresses, seersucker suits matched with starched white shirts and conservative ties adorning parents seeing off children, relatives and friends. The genteel natives moved, spoke and acted in the slow, soft, delicate modes of the courteous Southland traditions they were so imbued with. Toad felt warmed, relieved and comfortable in the familiar, restrictive, safe-haven these well-understood styles imparted. He was glad he wasn't adrift up north with the harsh unfamiliar attitudes of those uncouth foreigners known as Yankees. They seemed people lacking the decorum to attenuate their feelings to conform to others' subtle sensibilities. They lacked the charm and grace to shade the truth, that cold taskmaster that had a tendency to insult and shock the courteous, pleasant people to whom life was enough of a tragedy without the massive intrusion of a bunch of loud-mouthed smart-asses. Oh, the problems this war inflicted on the locals.

The youngster knew and felt the dark side of the people in his hometown, but over time, these attitudes which had shocked him in his prepubescent and adolescent years had integrated themselves into his psyche, and he had at last grown comfortable with them. He believed Houston's law and order was enlightened in its treatment of people. His father had explained years ago that Houston was not like the rest of the "Southland" because, as far back as the old man could remember, it had always been a crime to "kill a nigger" in Houston. He admitted that the crime only carried a ten-dollar fine, but went on to explain what a large amount of money that was in those days. The boy was once asked by his daddy, "What are you looking at?" and replied, "That colored lady standing on the corner." He was then subjected to a vehement and lengthy lecture proving his answer to this question was incorrect in the extreme. "There are no such things as colored ladies," he was flatly told, "only colored women."

Approaching the last coach, Toad found his assigned car and hopped aboard. The train was scheduled to leave in a quarter hour. He walked down the brightly-lit aisle, finally spotting two double seats facing each other near the middle of the car. After stowing his bag on the metal rack over his seat, he sat down facing forward near the window. His thoughts racing erratically ahead while peering into the dark cars nearby on the next track, he barely noticed Billy Bob in the aisle in front of him. This tall handsome youngster was a good-looking lad of 16 who had just started the university this semester. Toad recalled that he had met him last summer, and was impressed by his beautiful date but couldn't remember his name and attempted to ignore the young intruder's presence. The tall youngster, however, being no mind reader, approached, smiled and plopped down in the seat next to him.

Billy Bob waited patiently till Toad finally finished his ignoring gaze at the dark nothingness of the blacked out, olive drab passenger car sitting silently about a yard away from the window. Billy had his eyes riveted on the back of the other boy's head, and as Toad turned he said, "Hey Toad, remember me? I met you last summer when you were dating Jean. Man! How did you get her family so upset? She still expects to marry you before Christmas, and . . ."

He kept up the chattering gossip for some full twelve minutes. Toad had been observing him trying to figure out what tact he could take to get in control of the conversation, but found Billy's conversation had such an emotional impact on him that he could do no more than listen to these revelations in a sort of stupefied astonishment. Billy's ingenuous naiveté, unsophisticated candor and loquacious friendliness absolutely charmed Toad and from that moment the two became fast friends. They began conversing in earnest and scarcely noticed the other passengers that were boarding the train, taking their seats in the same car. Suddenly the train made a short lurch forward to begin a slow jerky acceleration on its way to Austin, the capital city of Texas and pride of Travis County. Within minutes, the clickety-clack of the wheels and the swaying of the cars gave Toad and Billy the secure feeling of power, speed and movement that seemed a thrust into the veiled future of their perceived destinies; tomorrow's impatiently looked forward to with optimism.

As Billy Bob went to the end of the car for some ice water, Toad glanced around the near empty coach to see who else was on the train. On his side of the aisle there was no one seated in front of him and only three in back. Slumped down just two seats back sat a dark, ill-clad, unshaven Mexican type with a new haircut. He looked like he'd been working all day, but his straight, dark, shiny, black hair was parted on the side and slicked down across the top of the broad crown of his head at 90-degree angles from the part. The sides were completely shaven almost to the curve of the crown where the thick, black, plastered down hair came to an abrupt end. He had the appearance of a poor laborer with that resigned and passively stoic look Toad had seen so often in these brown men pushing through their 40's and 50's.

Two additional seats back and reading a Sunday issue of the Austin American Statesman a white mustachioed and goateed southern gentlemen sat, immaculately coifed and dressed in a light blue-gray vest and cutaway coat. A light wide-brimmed plantation hat rode on the overhead rack above his head and a perfectly knotted black string tie lay under his heavily starched white collar. He was a tall thin ruggedly handsome old man with a smooth pink face. Toad estimated him to be about sixty-years-old. He looked like those old "Southern Colonels" he'd seen in movies about the Deep South. There seemed to him to be many movies of this genre made in Hollywood in his memory.

Billy Bob, returning from the front of the car with a small wedge shaped paper cup full of ice water offered it to his new friend, who tried to grab it from his hand as the coach lurched around a turn. Feeling the jostle, his reaction was to grip the cup tighter, which resulted in forcing half the cold liquid out of the cup and onto his lap. Toad jumped up, shocked by the cold, and quickly walked toward the bathroom for some paper towels to dry the excess from his now water stained khakis. He heard a grating laughter and felt humiliated by the tasteless remarks coming from two of the Air Force personnel he had seen earlier on the platform. They were now sitting across the aisle one seat in front of him. He thought them obnoxious, loathsome, and vile.

Returning from the men's room with a fist full of paper towels over and under the damp khakis he noticed for the first time the sweet countenance of a young blonde country beauty in her pale white pink flowered cotton dress. She was sitting alone in the double seat immediately in front of the two coarse, beetle browed soldiers, both of whom were doing their best to annoy the poor thing with their crude rasping innuendoes and vulgar attention. She was a picture of delicate decorum, of a chaste virtuousness almost angel-like, which when contrasted with the soldiers' lecherousness and satyr-like offensiveness, seemed absolutely pure and incorruptible. The sharpness of the soldiers' repellent and noisome tones were the only discordant sounds in the entire car, but the two youngsters didn't feel compelled to do more than make a few soft smiling comments to each other about "ugly, uncouth, loudmouth Yankee-swine," and ignored them as best they could.

Thirty minutes out of Houston, just before the lights went out in the coach for the remainder of the trip, both boys were still engrossed in their rapid conversation. They explored their amazing similarities and plans for the future. They were both stunned into silence by the sudden arising of one of the dark curly-headed airmen of particularly loutish appearance, and his rapid movement into the double seat where the pretty blonde flower sat. Within seconds he had his arm around her and began nuzzling her neck, creating a peculiar slobbering sound, which permeated the car. The two boys had just enough time to look with complete surprise into each other's eyes when the lights went off. It seemed as if they were still staring into the other's lit up face, for these last images seemed frozen on their retinas, as if locked into the fourth dimension.

Moon beams, lighting the small farms, pastures, and trees sped along with the swaying coach as the sonorous locomotive bore on westward through the quiet darkness of the Texas night. The boys drifted in and out of sleep with the faint background of smooching sounds oozing from the unlikely couple across the aisle and aggravating the otherwise soothing, syncopated rhythms of the train. There were people and conductors who moved intermittently down the aisle from car to car, and once around 3:30 the boys awoke, got themselves some more water, continued their modulated conversation a bit, and fell fitfully back into a near subconscious state closely akin to, but not quite, sleep. Then quite suddenly at five o'clock the glare of the lights illuminated every nook and cranny of the car as the conductor intoned, "Austin 30 minutes, Austin 30 minutes!" The bedazzled passengers began to stir and straighten their clothes, put on their shoes and move to more upright positions.

Once the few passengers in the coach regained sufficient use of their faculties to become aware of their surroundings, the only show in town was the smooching couple. They had stopped necking now, and in fact were both attempting to button buttons, straighten out ties; dresses and shirttails, combing hair and replacing make up. The soldier's face was seen to be covered with red lipstick smears when he stood up to tuck in his shirt. It seemed that everyone in the coach had their eyes fixed on the pair and couldn't help but notice, when, but a few minutes from the station, the smirking airman whispered something in the young girl's ear. Her face turned scarlet, and in less than a heartbeat her cries and sobs echoed through the coach. The two boys across the aisle were nonplused and felt quite uneasy at this turn of events. Still, they kept to their seats, not understanding the full implications of the scene they had just witnessed.

It was then that the white goateed "Southern Colonel" type slowly and deliberately rose up out of his seat and strode, ramrod straight, up to the crying girl seated beside the soldier, who had a somewhat surprised expression on his lipstick smeared face. The colonel's brow knit as he bent over at the waist and softly in a fatherly tone asked, "Pahdon me, Missy, but did this heah pusson ax youons to sell him youah body?"

"Yessuh! Yessuh!" she sobbed, and then almost as loud as she could, she screamed, "He offah me fie dollah," her voice breaking into a series of muffled soft sobs.

For the first time, you could see a look of shock on the old man's stern visage. He straightened up sharply as if struck, and turned his steely-eyed gaze to the contemptible, wide eyed and open mouthed airman sitting in front of him. As the despicable lout squirmed under the old man's withering gaze, the colonel's eyes burned with hate. His mouth splayed into a grimace of disgust, as he deftly reached into a lower left pocket inside his coat and plucked out a small chrome-plated, pearl-handled, two-shot derringer, which he pointed at the face of the cringing serviceman. Then, suddenly raising his voice, yelled hotly and with unbridled rage over the two rapid shots, *"This'll teach youah yunkee som bitch to try to raise the price of ayuss in Travis County."*

Silence fell like a blanket over the coach. Only the deep squeal of the train's brakes accompanied by strong muffled bursts of steam could be heard as the train decelerated to a stop in the Austin Station. The boys grabbed their bags and hopped off.

"I think we've just witnessed history." Toad said.

"How's that?" Billy softly replied, as they together rounded the corner of Congress Street.

"Why that Yankee he shot was white. I think race prejudice must be on the way out. Maybe the war is changing our traditions. What do you think?"

"Oh I dunno," Billy said, "Lets go to the Night Hawk and get a big breakfast. I got a four-bit piece."

"OK," said Toad, *"but don't it just make you proud to be an American?"*

THE SAD, SAD TALE OF QUINCY JOE

I abandoned him early one cool morning back in the early spring of '86 at a small motel in the southwest. It was almost an afterthought. I was forty miles down the highway before I realized the full implications of what I had done but only mulled going back for him about five minutes. The speedometer, gauging a steady 55 mph on cruise control, never varied and seemed to know right off that my answer would be no. Never look back! Never turn around! It was over and final! I was through! The relationship was finished.

I'm not sure what triggered my decision. I only know that early that morning, I saw him as he really was for the first time, misshapen, ugly and rotten through and through. I was disgusted with both him and myself, and the desire to run away, rid myself of him forever, flooded my senses. Quietly, I packed, walked out the door, started up the car and drove off without a word. What a sensation of relief! I felt free at last. I was happy and alive again for the first time in a long while.

Our relationship had lasted over twenty years, through some of the happiest, most pleasant days of my life. How handsome he'd been then, perfectly formed, tight in body with his typical expansive zest, looking like he would burst his seams. Clean! Warm! Straight! He had a perfect figure, a flawless form, just right for me. How I craved him then. What comfort he gave me, what bliss. His compliance was more than I could have wished for and his loyalty beyond question. Whatever I required of him, he supplied happily. I was proud of him then, and my step each day a bit lighter, a bit springier, because I knew he'd be there for me when I needed him. Of course, I bored my friends with my perpetual chatter, expressing my feelings of warmth and love for him, but I couldn't stop repeating those endearing words again and again. Even now I feel eternally grateful for those wonderful years. They will always remain part of me, a very special part, and a part I will lock up in my memory chest to take out and remember fondly till life's end and hopefully beyond.

Over these same years he had grown old, undependable with an erratic streak. Some nights I was never sure what shape he'd be in the next morning. Even last year after he had grown flabby, misshapen and careworn, unkempt and thin, Oh so very thin, I still adored him. Why did my friends get on my case? I don't know. It was no business of theirs. Why did I listen? When my friends questioned our relationship, I'd try to laugh off their unsavory remarks, their innuendoes, and their snickers. No one, it seemed, could say anything nice about him anymore. In fact, as time passed, their loathing became ever more slanted toward me. They began accusing me of having some kind of fear, of a paranoia for keeping him with me, and for continuing our relationship for all these years in spite of his physical decay. Oh I knew he was old, used up and ready for the dustbin. I suspected he had lived up his usefulness, his youthfulness, but I just couldn't toss him out like a frayed shirt or pair of torn trousers. Still, was it the time for me to find someone new, to change my ways?

I was in my fifties at the time but still carried myself well, still had my hair, felt young and looked the part. I'd kept in good shape and felt it, but I began to listen to them and believe I could find another.

"You've got plenty of years left," they'd say, "You need to get out and find a newer, younger match, one more presentable, one with a future."

Oh, I didn't listen at first. All these years that passed during our relationship had been wonderful, and I had never even looked at another. I never noticed the aging process that had taken place. I thought of him, as he was when we first met. His process of change was so imperceptible it seemed invisible to me. The idea of parting struck me as obscene. They just couldn't understand what we meant to each other, what loyalty meant. All these years in sickness and in health my bed was his and his bed mine. Never a crossed word had passed between us, and except for those occasions when my work kept us apart we were together. I loved him, I counted on him, I needed him.

Hey, I'm no saint. I traveled a lot in those years, New

Mexico, Louisiana, Mississippi, Arkansas and all over Texas, wherever the gas fields called me, wherever an aminol, methanol or sulfur sweetening plant was needed or might be used. Sometimes I'd trip up to Canada, over to California, sometimes Oklahoma, West Virginia or Michigan, and there were plenty of those one night stands in sleazy motels, but never once did they mean anything to me except to cut through my loneliness for home and Biddle. I never spent a truly satisfying night without him.

What will happen to him now? He can't do anything on his own anymore, can't even get around. He'll lie in that bed until the cleaning woman comes in and discovers him. What then? She'll inform the manager of the place for sure. A bit of time will pass, and it'll become evident I'm not coming back to get him, maybe a day or two. He's got no money . . . no visible means of support. What will they do with him? Hell I've got to quit worrying about him. They'll handle it because they have to. He won't know where to find me or how to search me out. He knows, like Thomas Wolfe, *"You can't go home again."* Jesus, these thoughts are too morose to handle. I've just got to think about other things. Wonder if I can pick up a case of that great Ste. Genevieve Chardonnay in Pecos County?

Some years have passed. I don't want to tell you how many, more than a few but less than plenty. My friends couldn't believe how I could be so cruel and heartless to abandon him the way I did. They treated me somewhere between a criminal and a person that lost his mind. Hell, it was their incessant banter that made me do it. Sometimes I believed they were right. Occasionally my guilt would crop up, but I simply can't blame myself, or I'll go mad. I just did what I had to do, and I had no way out. The time had come to act, and I did in the only way I knew how. He never talked with me again, and I never discovered his fate. For all I know he's living out in "LaLa" land with a Mexican dude or maybe up in Frisco in fairyland. Whatever . . . The thing I'm sure of is that there's nothing he'll ever do to reconstruct that crumbling wreck of a body of his. He's bound to be still wasting away like an HIV positive or gone for good. He was faded and soft, lumpy and thin years ago.

Hell, he's gone, and it's good riddance.

Some months came and went, and then one spring day I met Quincy Joe. He looked positively beautiful and new and young. He even smelled sweet and wholesome. He was compliant but not naïve, and seemed strong and full-bodied, clean-cut and handsome. Oh, he was going to be expensive. It was obvious that he was one of those top-of-the-line types. But what the hell, I could afford him. Will He like me? The thought intruded. I never cared, I never wondered, my ego wouldn't allow it. I simply felt like I was still a great catch . . . that I could do anything, that I knew everything, that I could handle life and all the bumps it had to offer. I was still the master of my fate, the captain of my soul!" Irresistible, irrepressible, unreformable and irreligious, that's me. It wouldn't be long till he was putty in my hands. Trouble was, I'd never had a handful of putty that didn't turn out to be a mess, and a mess hard to clean up.

Well, let me tell you how my old buddies took it when I first showed him off to them. That first night I had a party at the house. I had him positioned in the seat of honor, in my Ming chair under a small spotlight. When the guests arrived they couldn't help but notice him on their way past my early nineteenth century credenza. He looked like the "Prince of peace." Was I proud, a feeling I hadn't experienced in a long time. I could overhear the remarks from the crowd, "What style!" "What class!" "Remarkable demeanor!" "Perfect form!" He was the hit of the whole bash. By all appearances he was the beautiful, strong silent type. I hardly recall him speaking a word, and yet as small groups crowded around him admiringly, I could feel his haughty disdain for them and believed confidently that, although they may approach him closely, none would dare touch him. He put them off like a brilliant star in the heavens. He shone like a burning diamond with that inner-glow, a flame that blinded and warned to stand clear and not come too close.

As the days and weeks passed, I noticed a subtle change in my friends' attitudes, or at least some of their attitudes. Two of them became downright hostile at lunch one day. We were having Chinese at the Happy Warrior's and between the Hot and Sour soup and the Crab Rangoon I detected a sarcastic note in

Wally's voice. In an instant Bruce joined in, and before I knew it I was being roasted all over again about Biddle and excoriated over my love for Quincy Joe. Shocked and shaken I walked out on them before the main course was served. They had dredged up those trying times after my liver transplant, when Biddle had been my constant companion for over a full month. His faithful vigil was nothing short of extraordinary. He never left me alone, always by my side ready to help, ready to offer consolation and comfort, never leaving my darkened room of pain and anguish for even a moment. It was an act of complete love, absolutely unsordid. The very thought of it brought tears to my eyes.

I hurried home to Quincy Joe and sobbed out my painful experience to him. He understood completely, showing neither jealousy nor pain, only doing his best to console and comfort me. Our relationship was more than satisfactory for a year, maybe a little better'n a year. I was happy, contented. I was pleased with his performances, but it was there, growing in my mind like a malignant spider. The thoughts were truly subliminal at first. I was only just barely aware of them, now in retrospect, but within the next six months these pensive ruminations had become an irritating crust, a layer of distrust and apathy. Was he changing or was I? Something had gone wrong with our affair. The first concrete evidence I had came one morning when I awoke to find him on the other side of the bed. He was just lying there indolently, not asleep, but seemingly lost in his own thoughts. When I jokingly chided him about this, his response was complete and sullen silence, but I should have anticipated that.

Some mornings I would awake to find him out of the bed completely. Once I found him in the other room doubled up in a curious state. I have no explanation for this. It was bizarre and decidedly ungentlemanly. Hardly a thing I would expect from Quincy Joe.

Then yesterday morning the final insult! I awoke late to find Quincy Joe and my wife cuddled together in what appeared a state of ecstatic bliss. We had sharp words, and she informed me that she thought him exquisite, wonderful and just her style. She couldn't understand why I cared about him at all. In my sleep, she accused; I was throwing Quincy Joe out of the bed, exhibiting nothing short of complete disdain for his feelings and character. I began feeling sick to my stomach.

"He is mine now!" She said. "You can fend for yourself. It's just too bad that you left that no good, beat up, rotten and lumpy crony of yours in that small motel in the southwest."

Her high-pitched laughter clattered between my ears like the clashing of two large brass cymbals, and I was lost, broken, alone and rushed to the bathroom to throw up. I wanted to blame Quincy Joe for this mess, but how? It is an easy thing to love a pillow, but they are hard to hate.

THE "Z" FILE

Following the first modern sightings of UFOs in the late 1940's, a new style of thought, boarding on the bizarre, and once reserved for mavens of astrology, phrenology, spiritualism and the like, has steadily manifested itself. A growing number of religious laity as well as agnostics, atheists and other dubious and doubtful elements of humankind have converted to a belief that a break in the natural chain of evolutionary life on this planet occurred in the dim past. This break, they came to believe, was caused by the cohabitation[*] of aliens of other worlds with humanity's primitive precursors.

Ancient biblical writings seeming to confirm these beliefs are found in the Bible: Genesis 6:1, 6:2, and 6:4 as follows:

6-1. And it came to pass, when men began to multiply on the face of the earth, and daughters were born to them;

6-2. That the sons of God came unto the daughters of men that they were fair; and they took them wives of all which they chose.

6-4. There were giants in the earth in those days; and also after that, when the sons of God came unto the daughters of men, and they bare children to them, the same became mighty men which were of old men of renown.

Was this the first documented alien contact with earthlings? Do these ancient lines presage our true heritage from the gods who instilled our beings with that immortal soul so necessary for afterlife in a different dimension, a dimension other than the

---

*Editor's Note: <u>Cohabit</u>- originally a conjunction of <u>coitus</u> and <u>habit</u>, especially when implying a number of inhabitants engaged in habitual coitus. No mention has been found, to date, in extant historical records of either umbilical-chords or any other form of music.

ones humankind presently perceive and use? Does this inter-species fusion separate humankind from the "lower animals" of our planet? Yes, of course! Why equivocate when this significant evidence is so substantial and pervasive?

According to most anthropological and archeological sources, our large-brained species appeared suddenly. The earlier Fossil record reveals the brainpan was much smaller in all "Homo" species. These same sources cite many digs of exploration leading experts in the field toward the fact that our precursors had limited vocal talents consisting of very few words, mainly expressed in grunts and clicks of one sort or another, resulting in a limited vocabulary of less than ninety words. [*]

Biblical scholars believe that Exodus was written in a primitive Hebrew of fewer than 8,168.5 words many thousands of years after the time of Genesis. Because the language had no way of expressing a longtime versus a short time, the six days of creation may have taken hundreds of thousands of years. Besides, the story was actually written after having been passed down through the oral traditions of the clan or tribe for many generations.

It seems quite reasonable to assume that our bestial precursors had no words to describe aliens from outer space. They merely referred to them as "sons of gods" who descended from heaven to cohabit, fornicate and generally have their way with Earth's female population. After a normal period of "R&R" they took their leave to complete their mission of exploration of our solar system and other unknown points of light in the Universe. They left us the legacy of semi-alien offspring destined to become part of our DNA. This infusion resulted in what many now consider *"modern man."* Miraculously, this is similar to the manner which Captain Kirk of the starship Enterprise so unselfishly used to spread his seed around the Galaxy in future times.

---

[*] Of these, it was determined that three words referred to types of bowel movements, i.e., small, big and whopper

Egyptologists in a 1921 dig below the pyramid of King Zosar, considered one of the first if not the first pyramid ever constructed, uncovered a small shrine of papyrus reeds, goat hair and Nile fish heads of a rare, now extinct, but beautiful variety. The shrine is reminiscent in character to small shrines unearthed in England, Greece, southern France and the Levant. These shrines lacked the papyrus and fish-head motifs found in the Egyptian one, but they did contain many specimens of goat hair of various hues.

A number of thin, finely constructed gold plates, seemingly bonded together in the shape of an IBM Formatted, 10MFD-HD, Micro Floppy disk were found in a semicircular hole on the north floor of the Egyptian shrine, now known as "Z-1." These plates were pieced together in 1925 in the British Museum, but languished unfathomed. They were stored in the basement until uncovered in the late 1980's by a lone computer hacker, rummaging around the dark and dusty areas of Egyptian antiquities, looking for a small steel stele to steal. This turned into no steal, however, as the importance of this discovery apparently forced him back to his computer station. He spent the next nine years working feverishly day and night, attempting to construct a special slot into his computer for it to fit. After five years of tinkering to no avail, constructing disk readers, he finally realized he was trying to place the disk in upside down and had to renew his efforts. Another seven years of trial and error showed the data on the disk could not be stored in any file obtainable through the DOS prompt "C>." At this point the museum considered calling in the French computer wizard A. Cramez from Paris, but this decision languished in Whitehall for the next seven years, or early into the next century.

In the meantime, both Russian and Chinese agents had smuggled microfilm copies of the disk out of England and hand-copied it through some of the reproduction concerns in India. Much to the chagrin of their English counterparts, the Russians sent copies to Israel, Egypt and Switzerland for study. The Chinese mass- produced and put them on the open market as a sales gimmick to help promote sales of their new silk soled running shoes.

Then one Sunday morning in 2025 A.D., in the city hall of a small town in the Midwest, two unnamed computer hackers, working on a scheme to download the complete files of the Federal Reserve Bank made a startling discovery. They discovered that the data from one of the Chinese disks would pop up on their computer if typed in as *"File Z."* The translation follows:

"Z-FILE" TRANSLATION
STARDATE: 281.729.8294

Arrived third planet from a star sauna. Officers and crew revived from stasis complete. All present and fit for duty. All Officers: **Captain Nigel X., Subaltern Rigby Y., Captain Chumley Z., Commander Algernon Moncrief and Sir Winston U** were accounted for. The entire host of enlisted swine is also present and active, including the lethargic **Pheneas Cowper-Cloppers**, still suffering from the ghastly fumes he inhaled on Zigal two. His ashen, pallid and mealy coloration still causes him to appear as pale as a *"forpined ghost,"* whatever that is. An extra ration of food, water and underwear was issued according to regulation HD6295hy9 as the men had been in the stasis for over 45 light years. Plans are being made to begin a low fly survey of the planet following reclimatization.

STARDATE: 281.729.8296

Hovering at a constant 2,000' ASL we completed our reconnaissance traverses which covered 6,666.66 miles (actually called plinkos). We are presently studying our scans for details. Located various quadrupeds and bipeds, some of which we retrieved for the Barbie.

STARDATE: 281.729.8298

During our second group of traverses we found a clutch of gorrillyas, a bipedal mammal of vile and unspeakable habits. They have small heads, very large faces, odious bodies and exceptionally repellent looks. They were, however, observed to be extraordinarily fat and hairy, which prompted Captain Nigel X to comment on the fact that the saltpeter shots we took light years ago have lost their potency. The enlisted swine have purposely been kept unaware of the gorrillya development, and have only been shown pictures of the baboons and orangutans.

When the baboons began to gyrate in many directions at once, however the men glimpsed their colorful rear ends and became aroused and restive for the remainder of the night.

The wonderfully hairy bodies and corpulent, full buttocked frames of the gorrillyas, in spite of their repugnant, loathsome and disgusting qualities looked to the men as plump as dumplings. When pictures of them were shown to the assembled crew, a wave of desire seemed to overwhelm them, and the pictures had to be discontinued. According to officers' reports, the crewmen have been overheard making a number of salacious and erotic comments containing innuendoes of the foulest perversions. These included remarks alluding to pedophilia, bestiality, sodomy and other pleasant boyhood experiences, and indicate an unseemly level of concupiscence and pruriency in the crew, unheard of in prior excursions of exploration in past expeditions. I contemplate installing the proper disciplinary orders should these reports continue.

STARDATE: 281.729.8300

I dispatched Nigel, Rigby and five of the enlisted swine to the surface at 0800 hrs. Their mission will be to parley with the Gorrillya band inhabiting the bushy area of vegetation near the western, fringing seacoast of this Dark Continent, (coordinates: 37.526G, 71.775D and 101.111X). Their important duty will be to make our first contact with the natives of this land. I have supreme confidence in the officers' abilities to accomplish this task successfully, as both Nigel and Rigby have sufficient prior experience in these matters, albeit never with such repulsive, yet strangely attractive, beasts. Their strong command of the enlisted swine will also be tested on this duty. Sir Winston and I shall monitor their progress in this action from the safety of the ship, should unforeseen problems develop.

STARDATE: 281.729.8301

The dispatched crew reported on their return, flushed with excitement and overburdened with edible plants and fruit. In return for the gorrillya's largesse, Rigby presented them with some mirrors, glass beads and a few bright, copper coins bearing the likeness of our supreme sovereign, Queen Louis the Flatulent. According to Rigby, the gorrillyas seemed overjoyed with the exchange, and many offered their women for mating on the spot. Later this night Rigby and Nigel regaled us around the dinner table with tales of the girl's antics. There were evidently six extremely comely maidens in the group, all with beautifully lyrical names. According to Nigel the sounds of their names alone were enough to set one's mind aflame with desire.

There was *"MAGOOGA,"* the fattest, most beautiful and mature one in the group. Her aloof, cool and all-knowing smiles seemed to give her large face a shining, almost rosy glow. This unnerved the crew while she gazed placidly at our men   and slowly stroked herself between the legs. *"GAMOOLA,"* the saucy one, kept picking small sticks and bugs from her buttocks area and throwing them to the crew, while smiling, sticking out her tongue and moving her eyebrows up and down in a provocative manner. *"ENIGMER,"* the silent, kept her mouth open in a perfect *"O,"* her brows all squinched up in large attractive folds during the entire four hours of the meeting, an incitement the men were ill prepared for.

"LITTLE FORGNIA" was the shortest but hairiest one of the group. Nigel described her as constantly combing the hair on her torso with her long, oversize, dark fingers. At times she would gently twist the thick brown strands into cute little curls. She was almost as short and twice as wide as our officers and men. The coy looks she delivered to the enlisted swine were fraught with a deeper meaning that all could sense, actuating the men to become quite nervous with desire. *"ALAGMUS,"* with her flashing black eyes, frozen smile and lolling tongue was the picture of staid aloofness throughout the first three hours of the meeting. Everyone was quite impressed with her regal bearing. She then began to move slowly toward our troop and quite impulsively, licked the enlisted swine on various portions of their exposed anatomy while they stood rigidly at attention. Finally there was *"N'IGA-NINNY,"* undoubtedly the most spirited one in the entire pandemonium. She spent the entire time with hips undulating and rolling her eyes until some of the men fainted from the excessive emotional overload.

STARDATE: 218.729.8301.5

Later, in the privacy of my quarters, I reviewed the entire

proceedings from all angles on my holographic stage. I reached the agonizing conclusion that a stint of R&R on this enticing planet was necessary to avert an impending crisis. The potential of a crew mutiny has passed the critical point and may not be averted without allowing the men to blow off some steam. I decided to call a high-level command meeting with Sir Winston and Commander Moncrief to discuss procedures for disembarkation and personnel deployment for my proposed R&R program.

STARDATE: 281.729.8302

Sir Winston curtly informed me that he would be going ashore with the first contingent and blatantly refused to remain on board another hour, especially now that plans have been made for disembarkation. I reprimanded him harshly, stating that I, myself, anticipated leading the first contingent, and that I expected him to have the intestinal fortitude and rock-ribbed willpower to wait the few minutes and lead the second contingent. If he felt quite incapable of that, however, it should fall to his responsibility to pick the enlisted swine who would remain on board and watch over us until our safe return.

Algernon broke in. "There is a natural candidate for this task. It is none other than poor Pheneas Cowper-Cloppers."

"But why would you select that poor unfortunate?" Sir Winston asked.

"Right, Sir Winston," I agreed, I see no reason to select the unfortunate Pheneas to be forced to remain on watch while the remainder of the crew is on R&R. What possible reason do you have, Algernon, to select this blighted and hapless wretch for the task. It seems to me that you have made a completely heartless selection, which indicates a decided harshness to your overbearing nature."

"I say, old boy," Algernon said in reply. "Don't you recall that last night after your drinking session, when you finished two bottles and a pint of Camarian brandy, and had me incarcerate poor old Pheneas Cowper-Cloppers. You staggered out on deck and barfed on your dress whites. Poor, blighted Pheneas happened to be stationed on watch at this exact spot, and you accused him of committing this foul deed on your person. I had him clapped in irons and immediately hustled off to the brig on your command. The poor wretch still languishes there. It is quite a pity."

I bridled, rather hotly, and said, "But I remember quite well, Algernon, that I specifically told you to let him out the next morning. Why didn't you let him out? Why didn't you follow my orders? This smacks of gross insubordination. I must say, I am quite surprised, Commander Moncrief, that you did not follow my orders to the letter. Why didn't you follow my orders to the letter? I felt all along that you were somewhat apathetic and callous, but you have now proved it to me completely. I'm no longer sure you have the proper temperament for your position in the fleet."

"But you see, old boy," he countered, "We have him on another charge at present." He smiled almost smugly and snapped to attention.

"Oh well, what new infraction did the poor unfortunate commit now?"

"Sometime after I placed him in the brig I came back to your room to make my report, found you asleep on your bed and discovered that **he** had shit in **your** pants, unspeakable man that he is."

"Quite so, quite so." I replied, "It was a proper action you took after all. Capital, yes capital, Pheneas Cowper-Cloppers shall be placed on ship watch, while the rest of us pursue the arduous task of R&R on the surface. These proceedings are closed."

I informed the officers and crew of their leave status, assigning individual escape pod numbers for their personal use and allowing them to commence disembarkation on their own recognizance. Sir Winston and I departed for the surface in uncommonly high spirits.

**EDITORS NOTE: THE NEXT 16.785 MINUTES OF THE TRANSMISSION FROM THE DISK WAS GARBLED AND COMPLETELY UNDECIPHERABLE THE ONLY PHRASE THAT COULD BE MADE OUT SOUNDED SUSPICIOUSLY LIKE SOME INDIVIDUALS SINGING

"COKE SACKERS ON PARADE." (This phrase was not only unrecognizable to experts in the field, but also unrecognizable to laymen).

STARDATE: 281.729.3209

Piped aboard with all hands reporting save one. Preparations underway for space blast to clear us of this planet's gravity. Navigation is ready to proceed to the next star-saunas on our itinerary. The enlisted swine, with a few important exceptions have been placed in stasis for the journey. All of the officers' reports are in place, as this is expected to be my last log entry for the nonce.

Neither the Shandroydon Orgiastic Rites of springtime, nor the Glucosamites in their Full Flowering Sensual Flow could in any way compare with, much less match, the sexual fireworks accompanying our crews bonding with the quaint gorrillya lassies. I am quite simply incapable of the aphoristics necessary to fully describe the nauseously sticky, sweaty and corrupt aromas and piercing ejaculatory screams of ecstasy and delight emitted by both natives and crew on their joinings.

According to Rigby, who witnessed most of the proceedings, the crew and six to ten of the female gorrillyas began circling one and other, exchanging words and coy glances, and this continued for an indeterminable amount of time, as no one seemed to know exactly how to proceed. Suddenly three previously undetected females burst upon the scene in an amazingly erotic dance, sometimes bounding over *ten feet into the air* and electrifying the crowd with their unspeakable sensuousness. The three were later identified as the erotic **"MENIMIC"**, the graceful **"FATULINA",** and the completely amoral but enticing **"PHLEGMA."** Their Dance of the Toads lasted over thirty minutes to an hour, as the inflamed crowd lost all sense of time in their maddened rush into pandemonium.

Suffice it to say that this rush of savage love immediately dissolved into a scene of abject and overpowering abandon by both the participants and spectators. The dissolution was awe-inspiring to the point that I must admit, has no parallels in the historic annals of our race. The carnage consumed us all. It was only six days later when we gathered all the broken bodies, together with our overweeningly satisfied spirits, and drifted back into some semblance of reality. The very ground beneath our feet seemed parched and burnt by the heat of the occasion, as the officers and I began to search the rubble and realize the hideous toll these orgiastic rites had taken on both our psyches and souls.

There were, thankfully, only two fatalities, a fact that was a relief to both officers and men. I had feared much worse. Pheneas Cowper-Cloppers was mostly an unrecognizable mass of protoplasm, absolutely liquefied from the chest down to his ankles. Three eyewitnesses concurred that four of the maidens, in a possible fit of jealousy and desire, actually copulated, chewed, ripped and sucked his body to shreds in their beneficent outpouring of love, probably unlike anything previously experienced by the poor lad. Thankfully, all agreed he died in a state akin to euphoria.

"LUH BATARDO", one of the male gorrillyas, had sneaked into this area of love, (though all the males had previously been specifically forbidden to do so by their HEADMAN). He was caught delving into *"LITTLE FORGNIA"* by six of the enlisted swine, who in an overzealous, arrogant and imprecise manner tore the unfortunate BATARDO to bits. Thankfully the other injuries were unremarkable, though markedly real and real marketable as well.

We placed *"LUH BATARDO's"* remains in a small capsule and covering it with glass beads and small mirrors presented it to the HEADMAN with our complements, prior to taking our leave from the planet's surface. We retained Pheneas' remains, posthumously promoting him to Staff Sergeant, for recycling shipboard. Just how he came to be on the surface, following his assignment to remain on board, was never explained. After many fond adieus and pox vobiscums, we bade farewell to the gorrillya group, returned to the starship and secured. Prior to departure, our last act will be to transport copies of this disk to the surface with instructions on how they are to be preserved for posterity, many of which will, no doubt, be ours.

Having set a course for Glaucous Benervi, our next scheduled stop, we once more say to you of the future, "All our love and understanding for your continued development, and goodbye for now. However, if it turns out we are saying this to you of the past, be careful of what you wish for, you may get it. Especially if it's on a star, for afar is farther'n your heavenly father, and we'd rather you weather your heather and smather your leather, whether hither or thither, except for **HITLER,** who was a real **GISTARD,** and have a nice day."

The data from the "Z-FILES" ends here, but we should never forget what they did here. The heroism, grandeur and simple love that our forefathers presented to us gives new meaning to the expression, "THANK YOUR LUCKY STARS." And that's fortunate, as the old meaning has been largely forgotten. Unless, it turns out that time really exists. If not, have a nice day anyway.

THE CALIPH OF FRANKISTAN

"Sure, it's a great idea. I'll be ready in about fifteen minutes, but what about the kid?" Fanny asked.

"Hell, we'll just go by the school on the way and pick him up. His class'll be over in a few hours anyway. I think he wastes enough of his time with those schoolmarm yokels as it is. You want him to get a real education, don't you? Besides, he loves to watch those thoroughbreds pounding down the home stretch as much as us." Bud said, lighting a long, fat Havana.

"Okay, Honey, but this'll be the second time this week. You'll have to handle it with his teacher."

"Leave everything to me. I'll have him out of there in jig-time. Hell, the kid's a natural. He picked nothing but winners the last time out, and his teacher tells me he's a goddam genius in arithmetic."

Actually, at six, their precocious offspring was beginning to cut in on their free time. If they didn't pull him out now, they would have to leave the racetrack early to pick him up when school let out. He was an only child, and since Rosalita, their Mexican maid, recently ran off with the tamale-man, Fanny had not yet found a replacement that she felt suitable.

They picked up the kid around noon from his first grade class at Poe Elementary, and headed out to Epsom Downs, the pride of Houston's horse-racing establishment. Once they settled in their box, they cut the kid loose. They felt that kids needed unsupervised time to explore the world and grow-up fast. Besides, this arrangement allowed both them and the kid more freedom of action.

"Major! Major! I just spotted that kid headed for the paddock."

"Was he alone?" the Major asked, preening his handsome steel gray mustache and straightening his satin vest.

"As always," Max replied, his straw skimmer cocked to the right, just barely resting above the bushy black eyebrows that accentuated his ruddy complexion.

"Well, Max my boy, we have a bit of research to do. Come on, step lively now, young fellow, we must observe this youngster in the act and determine just what's what, who's who, and why's why. Harrump!" the Major said, realizing the inanity of his last phrase while his eyes rolled a bit and his face reacted the same way it did when he smelled something slightly off.

The unlikely pair arrived in the paddock area and stationed themselves in back of the small six-year-old. He was a nice-looking, small, thin and wan, brown-haired kid in short pants, standing on the white-painted, wooden paddock railing, his face very close to the horse's head in stall number three. The men had moved slowly up to within five feet of the kid; when he jumped down, moved over and climbed up on stall number four. The men silently approached again, but couldn't quite make out the whispering, seemingly urgent discussion between the youngster and the horse. The conversation appeared decidedly one-sided to them. Still, the number four horse, with all the animation of the thoroughbred it was, moved that massive head quickly until a big brown horse's eye was almost on the child's nose. The horse neighed, shook that big head a bit, its muzzle quivering up and down, showing off those large front teeth, and finally, with a slight shudder, took a step backward, raising its two front hooves off the ground in a jerking manner.

Intently watching the horse, the men failed to see the youngster move to stall number five. By the time they realized what had happened and moved over in back of the youngster once more, they were again mesmerized by the horse's antics and paid little heed to whatever the boy was doing or saying to the horse. This went on and on until the last horse had been "checked" by the boy. Now it was a well-known fact, by the regulars around the track that Max and the Major would do almost anything for a buck, legal or not. But now in late May, when the passionflower vines filled the area with their lavender lace and yellow-winged maypops, the men were in no mood to eat only peanut butter and jelly sandwiches. Beefsteak was more to their liking, but this staple delicacy of the Texas Plains cost up to 25 cents a pound, and twice that in the sleazy cafes in the area.

It was time they found a way to garner some jack, and soon. The last real payday they had was on Texas Independence Day, when they found a high-roller from Tyler, one who made his dough smuggling hot oil across to Louisiana. They had bilked the patsy out of forty-five bucks in a ticket-switch he never even noticed.

The pair had been hustling the tracks using every underhanded ploy they could think of to make a buck off any slow witted character available to them, but pickings had been quite lean in the past month, and they were desperate again, like most always. They kept betting on too many "Sure-things" that turned into nothing but character-builders in disguise; besides, as always, they found what builds character in some, just tears it down in others.

"I'd swear that kid is talking to those horses," the Major muttered as he and Max followed him through the crowd, "Go up and ask him who he likes in the next race, Max, and be snappy!"

Max came back in a few minutes and said, "Major the kid wanted to split a deuce on the nose of number six. I had to give him my last two-bits to get him to talk."

"Hmmmm, why hell's bells," the Major replied, checking his tout sheet, "that's the favorite, he's one to five. We could get that kind of dope from anyone in the park. No need risking any of our bobs on that nag."

"But Major, Sir, that tip cost us two-bits. We could'a each had a hot-dog for that! You gotta pay half, you two-bit chiseler, Major, Sir."

Meanwhile the kid went back to his folks and began trying to get his daddy to place a bet on number six.

"Sonny boy, sonny boy, now calm down, I'll buy you a ticket on who? Woodway, yeah Woodway. He's number six, but you'll never get rich that way my boy. Even if he wins you only make two bucks; hell my cigars cost two bucks. It's hardly worth walking down to place that kind of bet on that kind of horse. Here let me just give you the deuce you'd win right now."

The horses lined up at the starting gate after a small delay, getting the unruly few to settle down in their places. They're off! Rounding the far turn Woodway was lost in the twelve-horse pack. He was still there as they rounded the backstretch and headed home. Almost on cue, at least it seemed so to Max; the leading horses slowed and Woodway turned on the gas. He won by a nose.

"Yea! Hot Dog! Yippee!" Max screamed into the Major's ear as they stood in the front row of spectators pressed against the high cyclone fence next to the track watching the horses cross the line. "He won! I told you he'd win. I knew it! I knew it! You dumb ass! You dumb ass, Sir!"

Max never could bring himself to call the Major anything but Major or Sir. Even after all these years together, his Marine service in the "Great War" locked his psyche in thrall of the Major's rank, as bogus as it was. The Major loved this appellation; it bolstered his facade. He had never been in the army, but he felt he had some hereditary right to the title as he had all of his father's medals. His father had been a Major for many years in the Spanish-American War, and the long jungle fighting in the Philippines. The Major was a Junior and knew a Major's role well, managing to study the curt mannerisms of his old dad without picking up the foggiest clue to the meaning or honor of it all. He did know, however, that his title, its facade, and his wits were all he could use to keep Max in check when the younger ex-marine's temper exploded, and explode it did on many occasions. The Major's thick gray mustache, which looked almost waxed in its perfectly trimmed appearance, would twitch in fear when Max's blood began to boil.

"Luck, sheer luck. That horse didn't win the race; the others simply lost it." Major smirked haughtily. "Still, I feel additional study is due. Let's hightail it back to the paddock and reconnoiter the kid one more time. Just to show you I am fair, thorough, and have an open mind on any situation, including one as improbable as this."

Back they went, moving through the crowd toward the paddock area. They arrived just in time to see the small boy heading out of the area toward the ticket windows.

"Damn, Major, we missed him," Max hissed.

"No, no, Max, there he goes. Follow him! Catch him and hold him until I arrive."

Max collared the youngster in the betting line.

"Hey, Mister, let go."

"Take it easy, kid. No harm meant. I just want you to meet the Major. He was a hero in the Great War, and he wants to meet you."

"Okay, but let me make my bet first."

"You can't make a bet here. You can't even get up to the window. Give me your money and I'll bet it for you."

"No dice, Mister. I ain't giving my money to nobody. Do you think I'm stupid? Well, I'll have you know I'm in the first grade."

"Hey, here comes the Major. You'll let him bet for you, won't you? And, hey, I was a Marine; I wouldn't steal from a kid."

"Well, maybe it's okay."

"Major, this is the kid I told you of. Kid, meet the Major."

"Major Ashby, 69th Rainbow Division, at your service. What may I do for you, my fine young lad?"

Much struck by the Major's dress and bearing, the boy whispered something in the Major's ear and handed him a two-dollar bill.

"Certainly, certainly, my boy. I'd deem it an honor to serve a fellow American. On the nose, you say? Very well, step aside, if you please!" He spoke with command to the multitude around the betting windows, and moved through the crowd right up to the betting booth.

He purchased a ticket to win on Horse Number Two in the next race, presented it to the youngster with a flourish, and said, "There you are, Master Marvin. That is your name, is it not?"

"Why, yes sir, it sure is. How'd you know?"

"My boy, your poise and panache reminded me of Captain Marvin M. Martin, the most heroic and patriotic officer under my command. He won citations for bravery under fire during my victories at the Battle of Chateau Thierry and in the Argonne back in 1918. But do not let me delay you further. I'm sure you may desire to view the race. I hope to see you again, and soon. God bless you, my son."

With that, the youngster ran off into the stands while Max, pulling at the Major's coat urgently, remarked "The betting booth is about to close up. Put up our last fiver on Number Two. Hurry up, Major! Hurry up, you slow-witted dumbass, Sir!"

The Major deliberately took out his tout sheet and read the dope on Horse Number Two in the second race.

"Hmmmm, four to one, Desert Cat, a gray, a two-year-old gelding from the Stanhope Stables outside Louisville... Hmmmm ... A Gray? Max, you know I never bet on grays. They're bad luck even when you win. I've never had any luck on a gray in my entire life. I swore I'd never place another bet on a gray, 'specially our last fiver. Impossible; it's simply impossible."

"Don't worry, Major, let me have the five. I know how to get your curse off this gray."

"You do?" the Major asked, looking absolutely perplexed as he handed the five-spot over to the prancing Max, who now had one hand under the iron-barred opening of the betting window.

"Yeah, yeah, you old faltered son of a dried dip stick, you dim-witted, feeble old windbag, Sir! I'll place the bet on the horse! You won't have to be part of it!" Max yelled as he pushed the five through the opening and ordered a ticket to win on Number Twelve.

"Not Number twelve, Max, Number Two!" The Major screamed, his right hand now gripping the satin vest over his heart and dropping his gold-handled walking stick, which fell on his perfectly white spats.

Max blanched, pushed the ticket back through the ticket wicker and screamed at the ticket master, "I wanted Number Two, not Twelve, you dolt. You gave me a ticket on Number Twelve." He waited expectantly but only received his five-spot back and no ticket.

"Sorry, sir, no more bets. The race has started and the betting rack is closed." The green-painted, wooden sliding door slid down and the ticket master disappeared behind it, leaving Max red-faced in frustration. The two men walked slowly toward the track, Max sulking, but the Major happy to have his fiver back in his watch pocket.

They're off . . . Number two; Desert Trap takes the lead right out of the starting gate. His lead increases around the far turn.

Through the backstretch the gray is still five lengths in front. Still ahead, pounding down the stretch to home, he wins, going away, by seven lengths.

"You convinced yet?" Max sighed dejectedly, thinking of the big porterhouse and French fries slipping out of his grasp.

"There, there Max my boy," the Major replied patting him on the shoulder, "Into each life some rain must fall, besides there's always the next race."

Max brightened a bit and said," Yeah, Major let's get back to the paddock quick. By the way how'd you know the kid's first name?"

"'Twas sewed right on the inside of his collar, Max. It was just big enough to read without my cheaters. And now I'm sure you understand why I hate betting on a Gray. Something *bad always happens.*"

They tracked the kid and his picks through the next four races, managing to run their five spot up to eighty-seven dollars before the race day ended. What a celebration they had in town that night. Max and the Major took a taxi downtown, and after stopping on the way to put the bag on a quart of Kentucky "Bottled in Bond," sauntered happily to Scholl's restaurant and ordered the thickest steak on the menu. Afterwards they both arm in arm staggered back to their room in the Texas State Hotel to drink a bit more and plot their next moves.

"Although I find the strange proceedings of the day thoroughly inexplicable and scientifically incomprehensible, I am quite willing to admit that the kid is in some type of communication with the present horse population at Epsom Downs. The very idea of a human being finding a point of similar value from which to converse in any manner with a stupid beast as ignorant as a horse boggles the imagination, but facts are facts, and they are right before us to behold. Behold!"

The Major arranged pieces of the winning tickets and the remaining seventy-seven dollars of their stash on the chenille bedspread in front of Max with a flourish. Max, wide-eyed and grinning, nodded his head expectantly as he opened a fresh green pack of Lucky Strikes, pushed a dent on the pack's bottom below the torn off upper quarter next to the blue seal and watched as a few of the clean new cigarettes moved gently into view.

"Oh crap, Major, Sir. The kid has got it all right; he's talking to them horses. I know it! I got this feeling."

"Ah yes, dear Max, but are they talking back?'

"Gotta be, gotta be. How else can he pick all those winners?"

"So now my excited and kind hearted friend," the Major said calmly, twisting the end of that perfect mustache, "What do we do with this veritable treasure trove? How can we put our new found knowledge to good use?"

"Let's lay it all on the next winners in tomorrow's races and head north."

"Maybe so, Max. Maybe so."

That night as Max slept, the Major's thoughts became ever more caught up in his projections of the amount of money he would need to turn his life around.

"A new suit . . .no, two. A Packard with a radio and a rumble seat, maybe a small house in the country with chickens, definitely a flat in New York, and money, plenty of money, maybe as much as twenty-five grand. Maybe I could even be like the rich and live in the shade, sip scotch, and eat shiny food. I'd go up and see Sis in Kansas City, give her back the measly seventy-five I owe her, with interest. Then I'd show that skinflint brother-in-law how to choke on his words about me being a deadbeat... Might even get some presents for their kids."

The next three days found the pair around the paddock looking for "the kid" without any luck.

"His folks just didn't bring him to the races," Max said, "and I'm not sure if they came or not. I don't know what they look like or even where they sat. What if we can't find him again?"

"We must find him, Max," the Major commanded, "Leave no stone unturned, put your nose to the grindstone. His name is Marvin. Go find a kid named Marvin with well-heeled parents. This is imperative number one! Now, this is a command. Do your duty and with dispatch. Here is a fiver to cover your expenses. I want action and action now. Be about it and hurry on."

Max accepted the fiver and struck off in complete dedication, but as he exited the track, he realized for the first time that he had no clue as to how to go about his search.

"Damn Major big mouth," he spoke to himself, "Sir! How can I possibly find a kid named Marvin in a town this size? There ain't no way, but I've never shirked a mission in my life, and I don't want to start now. That Major must be goofy to think I can find a kid in a town like this. Where are all the kids? Hey. I know, I'll ask a taxi driver. Those smart-asses know everything about a town."

Max walked over to the first cab in line waiting at the entrance to the race grounds and asked, "Where's the kid named Marvin?"

"What's in it for me?" the smart Alec replied.

"I'll pay you to take me to him, Goofy," Max shot back.

"Hell, man, kids are mostly all in school today. Which school do you want to go to?"

"The one that Marvin is in, stupid."

"Look, mister, there's schools all over town. How'd I know which one Marvin is in? Besides, there's a lot of kids named Marvin here."

"Hell, I know that, sonny. Just take me to Mrs. Crawford's boarding house on Kress Street. I'll show you the way."

When the taxi driver said school, Max's brain clicked into gear like a large water-powered gristmill. Miss Emma Jean, the Maestro's daughter, was a part-time teacher and she could, he figured, put him on track. She followed her old daddy around the country to help make sure he had a good place to sleep and some decent food. She always was a bright one, had a degree from some famous college up north, and was sweet as cheap grape jelly.

Rumor had it that the Maestro was a virtuoso performer with the New York Symphony Orchestra. He emigrated from Germany after the war, and had performed in concerts of his own in Boston, Washington, New York and Chicago; occasionally even tripping out as far as San Francisco in the early twenties. He certainly clicked heels with the finest gentry in those towns and lived fancy in the big city until his life took a down turn due to racehorse losses and bad tips on the commodity market. He went so far as to try to cover his margins with loans from a notorious loan shark who extracted his final payment via a few well-placed blows to the Maestro's left mitten, the one he fingered his violin strings with. This unfortunate turn of events took the Maestro completely out of the music business, and he began spending his working hours strictly around the race grounds, where he curried thoroughbreds for a living.

Wherever the Maestro could find work at a track, Miss Emma Jean tagged along to help the old geezer out, praising the beautiful sounds of his violin when he played in his room after supper. Seems as if the horses and violin were all that kept the old Maestro from complete decline, 'specially after his wife left him when he dropped out of favor with the brokerage houses, music critics, and neighborhood retailers.

Max was only interested in Miss Emma Jean's knowledge of the Houston Public School System and told her his story about how he must find this Marvin kid, describing him down to a *"T,"* whatever that is. Miss Emma Jean was quite happy to have a problem to solve, something a little more provoking than four plus four. She spent a good bit of time with Max listing the seven or eight possible grammar schools in the Riverside, River Oaks and Southwest parts of town where youngsters in the first grade cannot only be hijacked out to the racetrack during school hours, but be called Marvin to boot. Suddenly it dawned on Miss Emma Jean that Dr. Oberholtzer was the superintendent of all the public schools and as such maintained a list of all the children in each grade in each school. The list was most likely in some kind of alphabetical order with schools and grades all attached. Now this was something even old Max could comprehend, except for the positions of the "J" and "Q", so Miss Emma Jean thumbed through the telephone book, found the address, wrote it down on a nice crisp piece of flowery stationery and sent Max on his way.

Max again felt a warm chemistry, and realized anew how nice it was to spend time with Miss Emma Jean. Although he knew he was almost twenty years her senior, her starched blouse, flowery skirt and fresh scrubbed look reminded him of younger and happier times back on the farm in Virginia before he decided to end all future wars and join the Marines. There was a wholesome young thing he had thought he was engaged to at that time, but when he returned after the armistice and looked her up, she was already the mother of two and locked up in somebody else's stable.

Strangely, Miss Emma Jean had always taken kindly to old Max in past encounters at the various race grounds on former occasions. There was a peculiar sadness in his eyes that she recognized and felt drawn to in spite of his lack of moral purpose. She knew times were tough, and it was a dog-eat-dog world where a man had to survive any way he could. IQs just didn't seem to have much to do with a man having enough food on the table and clothes on his back.

Max returned to the hotel room that night and smilingly told the Major that Marvin was in the first grade at Poe Elementary. The kid could be picked up without too many hassles any weekday at fifteen hours. But because the races started at thirteen hours, he believed Miss Emma Jean should pose as the boy's Mother, Aunt or Maid around noon and promise him a good time at the races for the day.

"This calls for a perfect plan and consummate strategy", Major said, his eyes squinting, while twirling his mustache, *"but I'll figure the logistics down to the lick-log. My friend, 'twas a fine action you have managed this day. As fine a piece of work as the charge up San Juan Hill."*

Getting the kid to the track seemed a minor problem to the Major, but finding a partner with a large enough stash of ready money to follow his leads and split the gains squarely, there was a task worthy of anyone's best efforts.

For the next week and a half, the Major, discreet to a fault, tested his perceived quarry's potential with zero results. Crazy Moe, who would bet on which of five flies would first go airborne, thought the scheme too risky. Snigger the Shark was temporarily strapped for funds, having sprung for an interest in the newly decorated "Chicken Ranch" outside of La Grange. Fats Wooley claimed he had already bit on the same scam three years earlier at Belmont. Shifty McCoy had some religious scruples against the proposal. He said it was against his religion to bank on anything he couldn't have complete control of from start to finish but offered the Major a role in a particularly attractive heist of the Krupp and Tuffly Shoe store on Main Street. Even Sincere Smith turned the Major down, saying that he had promised his dear departed mama that he would never listen to a word a horse said, even if it spoke to him with an Oxford accent.

It was a few days later, when the Major was dejectedly wandering near the green and white painted row of horse stables, racking his brain for new prospects, that he heard the unmistakable strains of "The Great Fugue" by Bach. How beautiful it sounded to him on the violin. Quite different from the dark, chilling, almost grotesque sounds of the organ on which he'd generally heard it played in the past. He followed the sound and found himself standing in front of a horse stall. He looked across its straw-covered wooden floor and saw a three-year-old coal-black filly named Noteworthy Sue and her decrepit old groom bowing a shining violin.

The Major waited silently for the music to end, and end it did, abruptly in mid-passage, a complex one at that.

"Good Morning Maestro. That was a moving piece of Bach. The notes were actually vibrant and singing to me. Astounding, astounding music. I didn't know you still played and so well."

"Vot! Mien Gott, Major, iss it you? I do not know you vass dare. Yah, yah, it vas playink, but I vas not makink moosica. Only him, 'Caliph uff Frankistan' makes moosica."

" Why, who's that? Who is the 'Caliph of Frankistan?'"

" He iss diss!" The bent old man replied, holding his violin aloft with a flourish. "I luff it mit all mien heart, more den anythink, although Miss Emma Jean, Und vitch I must neffer part. It iss diss Stradivarius mien uff great walue. Years ago ve make bootiful moosica togedder." His low, wavering voice quivered slowly, and his old eyes glistened with tears as he gently laid the violin into the tattered, dirty, black case lying on a rustic wooden bench.

The Major saw the straw dust glisten in the shaft of sunlight shining through the open upper portion of the stall door, as the

Maestro shuffled through the hay covering the creaky floor. He thought for a moment that the "Caliph of Frankistan" looked like pure gold as it hit the light before disappearing into its dark case.

"Ever heard of a kid that could talk to horses-----," he began.

"Major! Major! I just spotted the Kid heading for the paddock," Max panted, his ruddy face flushed with exertion, sweat glistening in his dark eyebrows.

"Like manna from heaven. What a fortuitus circumstance!" The Major sighed, smiling, "Hotfoot it around to the barns and find the Maestro. Bring him to the paddock as fast as you can."

Some days before, he had promised the old man a preview of the action before he had to commit. It seems the Maestro was also an "equine communicator" or whatever one's called who has some method of understanding horses. When he was a youngster back in Bergedof he was an avid race fan and went to Hamburg as often as he could. In younger and happier days he felt a certain kinship with these German nags, and claimed he picked up quite a few Marks betting on them.

Before the third race the three watched the kid's antics as he moved from horse to horse whispering in their ears. They watched in awe as each horse displayed an agitated reaction to the kid's urging. They checked the kid's picks and were over three hundred simoleons ahead of the game after the next three races. Needless to say, by this time the Maestro was completely convinced.

On the phone that night the Maestro worked out a deal with a Chicago University Music Professor he had known briefly in the past who always wanted to strike a deal for *"The Caliph."* The Professor agreed to find him a loan for two weeks for twenty-five grand, *"The Caliph"* being the security for the dough. This same professor was an acquaintance of a certain Chicago Italian-speaking individual with very deep pockets, whom he had solicited funds from on other occasions for Symphonic, Operatic and other civic causes having to do with matters of music.

This "Don" was actually quite interested in securing a "Strad" for a certain party that resided in the Vatican. The professor had vouched for its authenticity, and "Strads" were hard to come by, especially for this price. In fact, if this particular Italian-speaking individual had known that an elderly ostler in Houston was in possession of one, he would have arranged for a nocturnal change of possession some time ago. He planned to dispatch two of his best and most trustworthy henchmen with the money to Houston to make the exchange as soon as possible. To be brutally frank, this Italian-speaking individual had no intention of ever allowing the return of the violin to its original owner. He felt the transaction would be of such a personal nature that word of it could be silenced sufficiently, should payback ever actually take place, and he felt the odds on this a comfortable 23 to one. He had a number of exceptional dispensations to request from the Holy See and felt this "Strad" would lubricate a specific sticky part of the mechanism.

Back in Houston, Max had been escorting Miss Emma Jean to dinner each night. They would stroll down Buffalo Drive savoring the cooler breezes in the evening, stopping to gaze into the store windows in front of the Sears and Roebuck department store before making each evening's final approach to their favorite steak house on Buffalo Drive. This night, much to his distress, Max noted how sad she seemed to be while they were in the middle of their dinner. In fact, now that he thought of it, Miss Emma Jean seemed to be getting sadder and sadder as the week wore on. This began to upset Max more than less and quite a bit as he viewed, after each bite of Porterhouse, how Emma Jean would start sniffling and daub her dainty handkerchief at her now reddening eyes. This especially bothered him, as he knew the horseradish sauce Miss Emma Jean spread liberally on her steak was much too weak to serve as an elicitor.

"Pardon me Miss Emma Jean for asking you what may seem to be a highly personal question right in the middle of your supper. Especially when you have just taken a rather large bite of steak, but in this wonderful world of plenty, beauty and happiness, just what seems to disturb you, and cause you such unhappiness when you eat this porterhouse steak with me every night? Is there something lacking in the food, service or company? Would you like some more tea, Lea & Perrins, or A-1 sauce? Is there anything I can do?"

"Oh, I am so sorry Max," she replied, "But the thought that my dear Papa, whom you call the Maestro, will have to part with his beloved violin for even one night makes me feel terribly sad. Besides in this particular arrangement, I fear that if he does part with it he will never see it again. I fear the Italian-speaking gentleman from Chicago may never return it, and this, I know would do my dear Papa irrevocable damage in the mental department. This, my dear Max, is why I cry a bit all the time. It is definitely not the horseradish sauce, which is particularly weak tonight.

"No amount of money that he might win on the horses can make up to him for so great a loss, and because of this I seem to cry myself to sleep most every night. The only thing that keeps me sane is the thought of going out with you and eating porterhouse steaks with horseradish sauce. You have become the one thing I love in life along with the porterhouse. Even when the horseradish sauce is weak as it is tonight."

"Miss Emma Jean!" Max replied emphatically, a lump he thought he'd lost many years ago arising in his throat. "I too am in love with you, you mean everything to me, and I promise that whatever happens, the Maestro, your Papa, will not lose the 'Caliph of Frankistan'. I believe in 'Semper Fi.', and my darling, Miss Emma Jean, you must believe in it and me too."

When Max, the Major, and the Maestro made their plans for the exchange, Max volunteered to be in the lobby of the local police station and physically tender the Caliph in its case at the appointed time. It came off without a hitch, although the grizzly pair from Chicago insisted on examining the contents of the old tattered case before handing over the fifty crisp five hundred-dollar bills.

The twenty-five "G's" in hand, the Major pushed his plan into high gear. At noon the next day Max and Miss Emma Jean picked up Marvin and, stopping for *"Coneys to go."* at James' Coney Island, escorted the youngster out to the track. They had promised to give him a sawbuck to bet on each race and bring him home after the last race of the day. Marvin was extremely happy with the arrangement and the deference they showed him.

The horse Marvin picked to win the first race was posted at four to one and the Major and Maestro bet twenty big ones on his nose. He won by four lengths. They huddled and decided to set aside the twenty-five grand for return of the Caliph, but when Marvin picked a light chestnut filly that was 10 to one in the second race they laid out 65 grand on her nose. It was a mile-long race and Chilly Lily, their horse, was running dead last at the quarter-mile post. At the halfway mark she was in the middle of the pack and broke into the lead on the final turn. Down the home stretch she was running neck and neck with the favorite, Blue Burnish, and won by a half-length. Pay was posted at $17.35 for a $2.00 ticket.

In just two races the group had won in excess of a half million dollars and were already getting quite nervous. They just weren't prepared for such success, and when Marvin picked an even-money favorite in the third race they decided to sit it out and prepare for the fourth race. They discussed splitting their swag then and there, but when the favorite, Sir Roquefort, won the race by six lengths, they decided to put it all up on the next race.

Marvin picked a horse named L'eminence Gris, an eight-to-one shot in the three-quarter mile fourth race. His odds dropped to three to one after the group placed over $200,000.00 on his nose but won the race by two lengths.

This was more money than they had ever seen up close. Even more than the Maestro envisioned during his virtuoso performances. They unanimously agreed to stop all betting and divvy up the jack fifty-fifty, the major and Max splitting up one half and the Maestro and Miss Emma Jean the other. But when they told the kid they were closing shop for the day and taking him home, he put up a beef and howled how they promised him a full day's outing, which he considered to be at least seven races. He began calling them cheaters, welshers, kidnappers and a number of other things designed to bring them under the attention of the crowd, a spot where they had no desire to be, as anyone carrying around a big pile of dough knows. The Major grabbed the kid. He clamped his hand over the kid's mouth and smiling began saying things to the gathering crowd. He spoke soothingly, trying to be calm. "O.K., Honey boy I'll get you an ice cream cone and a hot dog and a soda water," and anything else he could think of while he carried the screaming kid over to a far corner under the stands. Following was Max, Miss Emma Jean and the Maestro all trying to assuage the youngster's feelings. Max and the Major began to argue over what to do, while Miss Emma Jean took the bawling kid aside to dry his eyes and say encouraging words to settle him down after his little leather-toed brogans had found the Major's shins with such devastating effect.

"Listen, you old windbag, Sir, we promised the kid a day at the races and he is entitled to that for changing our lives around. We can't go back on our word to a minor, 'especially one that has helped us out like a real champion. Only a no-good lying crook like you would do a crummy thing like that, Major, Sir. No disrespect intended."

"Very well, very well, Max, my friend. The Major knows quite well how to handle situations of this nature. Where is the lad? I'll offer him fifty bucks. You just watch him snap it up."

"Marvin is over there under the stands with Miss Emma Jean, he's crying tears big as horse pops."

They approached the kid crying in the arms of Miss Emma Jean where the Major offered the kid a fifty on the spot, but this only made the kid cry all the more.

"You promised me a full day's action," he sniffled, "and now you're trying to renege, sob, sob. I thought you were my friends, choke, sniffle, sob, sob. I'm trying to run my stake up to a grand so's I can buy my own horse to take home and you offer me a lousy fifty bucks, boo hoo," he said.

"How far are you from reaching your goal, little Marvin?" Max asked.

"Only eight hundred eighty five bucks, sniff, sniff," the kid blubbered.

"Indeed!" said the Major "Well I'm not about to shell out all those potatoes for some broken-down nag for this kid. However, I see no great injunction to leave prematurely. The Maestro and

I will wait in our box in the stands while you and Miss Emma Jean help with the lad's betting until he runs his winnings up to where he wants to get them. Come, Maestro, let us sortie up to our seats, where we can enjoy the excitement of the remaining races while sipping mint juleps. We can contemplate the future in comfort like the patricians we are."

In no time the Maestro and Major were in their box seats sipping those juleps in high spirits and cheering for each of Marvin's winning horses without even making a bet on any of them. They had vowed separately and to each other that to make other bets would serve no purpose, they had achieved more than they thought possible and had only to savor their victories. They never even felt the oppressing heat and humidity as they laughed and contemplated the life of luxury they were now able to lead.

Major and Maestro might have felt a pang of regret now and again at the end of each race, 'specially when Kattegat paid four-fifty to one, but within a few seconds they would resume their self-satisfied banter and down another sweet mint julep. They only paused to check the full brown paper bags containing the cash at their feet.

"Mebe I go to Florida and do de schvimmink mit some young vemminks, mebe play mit dere shmegagees. Yah! Yah! But bet again. No! Neffer! It vould be mashugah."

"Absolutely, my dear Maestro, absolutely. A bird in the hand is worth more than two in the bush," Major said, but suddenly wondered if it was also worth four and a half in the bush, and with little Marvin doing the picking, could they truly be considered in the bush?"

Slowly, the afterglow of their success seemed to paltrify a bit, but they ordered more whiskey and smiled at each other in genuine pleasure. Then, just before the last race Max reported the kid's last pick; a two-year-old gelding named Charlemagne at five to one. The Maestro, drinking his fourth mint julep, started choking and coughing, and as the other two men pounded on the old man's back, the Major yelled at him.

"What's wrong Maestro, what's wrong?"

"Dot's der name uf mien Strad, mien 'Caliph uff Frankistan.'

It iss dur oriental name uff Charlemagne. Dis iss un sign

178

from Gott! Max! Help me to der bettink booth! I'm bettink mit mein all on Charlemagne on der noses."

The two took off swiftly for the betting booth with the Major running after.

"Me too! Me too!" the Major cried as he followed the pair. "We have to hurry to make it before they close."

As the four adults and one child seated themselves to cheer Charlemagne home, the horses were parading toward the starting gate. Charlemagne was horse number five and had green and tan colors, but the Major took one look and started a low moan.

"It's a goddamn Gray. Ohhhhh! They're unlucky. You can never tell what they're going to do. Kid, what makes you so sure he's gonna be the winner?"

"It's easy as pie," the kid said, his face beaming with all the innocence and confidence of youth, "I just ask all the horses in the paddock, and they tell me which one they are going to let win. Every horse in the race has already decided in advance, and I talked to every horse in the paddock. Number five can't lose."

"Well, if that don't just beat all," said Max his mouth agape.

"I still don't like it," the Major repeated, "There's never been a dependable Gray."

"Gallant Fox was a Gray," Miss Emma Jean said matter of factly, "and he won the Kentucky Derby."

"Yah, yah, dot's right. Vhat you bad talk Charlemagne like dat for, you Mr. Pig-mouth?" The Maestro yelled, "Now don't jinx mein own horse Mr. Major or ve're all mahoolah."

They're off! Charlemagne broke to a two-length lead right out of the gate. He was ahead by five lengths down the back-stretch. Rounding the near turn and heading home he maintained a five-length lead on the others.

Simultaneously, or there about, the Chicago pair arrived at the crowded railroad station in downtown Chicago. They called the Don and were instructed to drive to the Music Building at Chicago University to present the "Caliph" to a certain music professor who would be expecting them. He was in his office when the pair presented the case to him. He opened the case, lifted the violin out and for a fleeting instant thought he saw a Stradivarius label. He began searching for a telltale unevenness of the purfling and ropiness in the Bosnian Maple backside, but although the backside was maple, it showed little spontaneity and few areas of ropiness, hardly what he remembered. He wasn't sure, it had been years since he had played, held and studied it. He checked the ruggedness of the scroll. *"This doesn't look right."* The "F" holes next drew his attention. They were completely off. Neither Antonio nor his sons Omobono or Francesco could have cut them. Something akin to panic began to flood his senses. This looked like one of those Sears-Roebuck knockoffs advertised as Stradivarius replicas for $1.95 apiece.

The professor knew he was in a spot. He had vouched for its authenticity, the owner's authenticity at any rate. The Don would be furious, and who knew what he'd do. The prof needed time to think, but his panic was blooming more and more. The prof insisted in taking the violin to a quiet room to play and make a decision. The hoods didn't like it, but after checking the room out in advance allowed the prof to proceed. The one called Pattillo entered the room with the prof while Carmine guarded the door from the outside.

Almost as soon as the bow touched the strings the professor knew the horrible truth, and his panic blossomed infinitely. He had to keep playing, to stall while he conjured what to do . . . to say. His heart was racing faster and faster, and his music became louder and louder. He wanted to sit and stop, but he was terrified, he couldn't think. Pattillo yelled at him to quit the playing and make a decision, but the professor ignored him; with ashen face he began to choke, cough and gag. Suddenly the old professor's eyes glazed, and he faltered, the music stopped. Pattillo, standing by the door, rushed toward him, attempting to grab the violin, but only succeeded in forcing the fragile instrument from its perch on the gagging man's shoulder to his chest. They both collapsed to the floor, exploding the violin to bits under the weight.

Panic was suddenly Pattillo's problem, but he knew how to squelch it. He gingerly plucked the crushed pieces of splintered wood from under the stricken professor from whose head blood flowed in an ever-expanding circle. Should he try to explain this to Carmine, the cops, or the Don? None seemed particularly happy scenarios. He walked slowly to the door and told Carmine to call the Don and tell him everything was O.K., "The Professor agrees we have the 'Caliph', and get me some coffee from that joint on the second floor while I settle things with the Professor." As soon as Carmine disappeared around the corner, Pattillo sauntered out to the car and headed south.

Back at the track Charlemagne was headed down the home stretch in a five-length lead over the pack of horses that were strung out almost nose to tail except for Slappy Freight who was bringing up the rear seven lengths in back of the last horse in the pack.

Running full tilt down the stretch, forty yards from the finish line all alone, the Gray seemed to wobble and veer just a bit. Suddenly he took a left turn and crashed right through the inside wooden railing barrier and kept running in a broad circle. Then the unbelievable happened! The entire pack of horses followed him through the break in the railing until the track was entirely cleared of horses. It was then that Slappy Freight rounded the turn and all alone ran across the finish line. The track emptied. Emma Jean and Max drove Marvin home while the Maestro and Major fitfully devolved from their awake nightmare into the true dreamland of an alcoholic slumber in one of the empty horse stalls.

All the way home Marvin complained about horses as a group. Even though Charlemagne had already been diagnosed as a victim of severe infectious equine encephalmyelitus, Marvin still swore he would never bet on another horse, that they were never anything but a sorry passel of lying rascals who could never be trusted. He never mentioned his experience to his parents, who were across town in a poker game and never noticed his absence.

By noon the next day the Don had the situation all figured out. The Caliph was destroyed beyond all recognition and repair. People from Miami to New York to L.A. were on the lookout for Pattillo who broke the professor's head and killed him trying to put the hook on the *"Strad."* There would be no special dispensation this year without a large outlay of bucks.

He could live with it, but what if the old Kraut repaid the

loan and wanted his violin back? This was something he couldn't stomach. He was the responsible party, everyone in the country already knew what had happened with Pattillo: they would all lose respect for him. It would simply look too bad for him to go back on his word now; the news would spread through the underworld in a flash. He had to nip this in the bud and fast. He had his secretary write a personal note to the Maestro canceling his debt and enclosing a check for twenty-five G's. He explained the accident, asked for the Maestro's pardon and hinted that if ever the Maestro required a divorce in Chicago he could fix it up. There was also a veiled reference that his family would come under the Don's umbrella for the rest of his natural life.

The Major and Max had both squirreled away a few thousand each and decided to move to a new track for the fall season as the very sight of Epsom Downs choked them up rather badly. Before they left, however, Max said goodbye to Miss Emma Jean and told her how he'd switched violins. He gave her a key to a large safety deposit box in the National Bank of Commerce on Main Street.

"It's a much nicer case than that old torn one your dad had before, and it even has some real nice lettering on it saying how it is a genuine Sears & Roebuck Stradivarius. I knew that dumb, blowhard, ignoramus of a Major, no disrespect intended, would find a way to queer the deal."

Miss Emma Jean and Max embraced, kissed for a long time, and she told him she loved him and would be waiting for him at some race grounds, someday, somewhere. Max said she wouldn't have to wait too long, wiped his eyes, and slowly disappeared into the warm, humid night.

ABOUT THE AUTHOR

The author, C. A. Chimene, now follows his first book, "Hot Nights in Houston," with this "completely different" anthology of his best comedic writings. He establishes a broad-ranging talent through the comedy, irony, satire and pathos of his characters and narrations. His unique way with words breathes life into the fabulous tales he lays before you, and together, with his senses of timing and humor, should have you rolling in the aisles.

Though most of his stories have a decided Houston, Texas flavor, mirroring his hometown, he goes completely "around the world" with these tales. He belongs to the fourth of six generations of Chimenes that have resided in the "Bayou City." A veteran of WWII, he graduated from Lamar High School, the University of Texas, in Austin, with a BS in Geology, and received a Master of Science degree at the University of Houston in 1952. Chimene worked for Major Oil Corporation as both an explorationist and an executive until 1985 when he retired, started writing, and took over the reins of his family corporation. He now spends leisure hours at his P.C. tapping out poems, short stories, essays and novels. He is presently near completion on three more books and promises to have them in print in the near future.

He now likes to talk politics, religion, baseball, and football and tell jokes, but he is, of late, trying to conquer his lifelong infatuation for the opposite sex. Still, he admits he can "be had."